Tell Me About

FESTIVALS of India

ANURAG MEHTA

VANEETA VAID

Nita Mehta PUBLICATIONS

Tell Me About
FESTIVALS
of India

First Hardbound Edition 2005

ISBN 81-7676-042-0

Illustrations: Nita Mehta PUBLICATIONS

Artist: Rajesh Prajapati

Printed at:
BRIJBASI ART PRESS LTD.

Distributed by:
THE VARIETY BOOK DEPOT
A.V.G. Bhavan, M 3 Con Circus
New Delhi - 110 001
Tel: 23417175, 23412567; Fax: 23415335
Email: varietybookdepot@rediffmail.com

Layout and laser typesetting:

National Information Technology Academy
3A/3, Asaf Ali Road
New Delhi-110002

Published by:

3A/3 Asaf Ali Road, New Delhi-110002
Tel: **91-11-23250091, 29214011, 23252948, 29218727**
Fax: **91-11-29225218, 91-11-23250091**
E-Mail **: nitamehta@email.com,**
snab@snabindia.com
Website : http://www.nitamehta.com,
http://www.snabindia.com

Contents

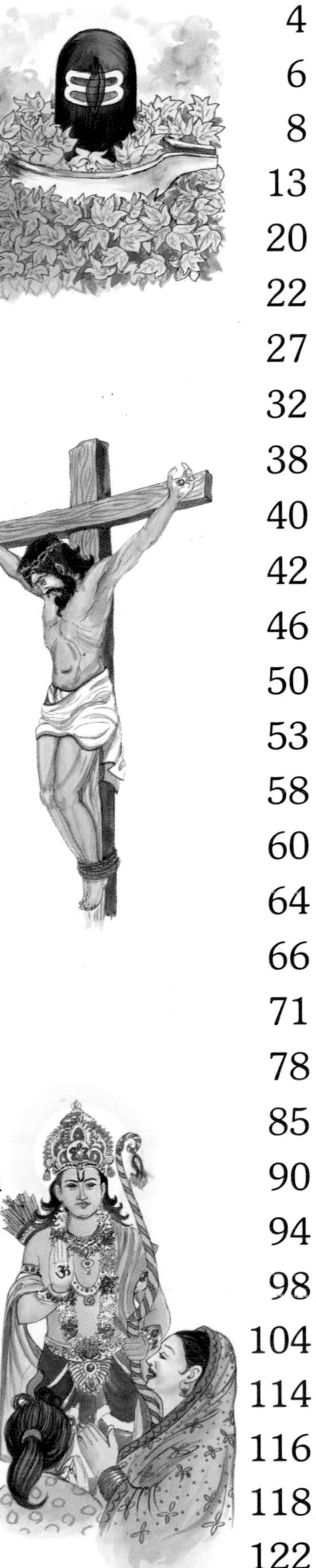

Introduction

India is one of the most culturally diverse countries in the world! As India is a society of many religions, we celebrate many festivals too. Almost every day of the year, there is a festival celebrated in some part of the country. Some festivals welcome the seasons of the year, the harvest, the rains, or the full moon. Others celebrate religious occasions, the birthdays of divine beings, saints, and *gurus* (revered teachers), or the advent of the new year. A number of these festivals are common to most parts of India. However, they may be called by different names in various parts of the country or may be celebrated in a different fashion. Festivals in India are characterized by colour, gaiety, enthusiasm, prayers and rituals. Whichever corner of the country anyone is, festivals are celebrated with gusto! No wonder, India is rightly described as a **land of festivals!**

Apart from various religious and seasonal festivals, there are some important national days that all Indians celebrate with pride and joy. These are the **Republic Day**, which falls on the twenty-sixth of January, **Independence Day** falling on the fifteenth of August, and **Gandhi Jayanti** falling on the second day of October. Different festivals occur according to the calendars followed by different religions, though some festivals do occur on fixed dates every year.

CALENDAR

The word 'calendar' means an accounts book in Latin. A calendar divides a year into months, weeks and days. The **Roman calendar** is used all over the world which is a solar calendar. This means it is based on the movement of the sun. According to this solar calendar, there are 365 days in a year and 366 every four years. The other two main calendars, also used in India, are the **Hindu calendar** and the *Hijri* or the **Islamic calendar**.

HINDU CALENDAR

This calendar is based on the lunar cycle of months, which starts from one full moon day to the next full moon day. There are 12 lunar months. The lunar calendar consists of 354 days, which is 11 days less than the normal calendar of 365 days. Thus, every 2-3 years one extra month is added to the Hindu calendar, which is known as the *Adhik Masa*. The names of the months of the Hindu calendar in order of occurrence are *Chaitra, Baisakh, Jyeshtha, Aashad, Shravan, Bhadrapad, Ashwin, Kartik, Margshirsha, Paush, Magha* and *Phalgun*. Each month is further divided into two fortnights called *Paksh* according to the movement of the moon i.e. its waxing and waning. The fortnight following the new moon night is *Shukla Paksh.* Full moon night is called the *Krishna Paksh*. The festival days are determined according to their occurrence, such as the fifth day after full moon day or otherwise. That is the reason why almost all the full moon days are auspicious days.

HIJRI

The Islamic calendar is also a lunar calendar for it is based on the movement of the moon. A new month in *Hijri* starts only when three responsible people sight the new moon and then it is endorsed by the head of the main mosque. Therefore, the exact date and days of the calendar month are not fixed. For example, normally a month is of 30 days, but if the moon is sighted on the twenty-ninth day, then the new month would start from that day itself. The festivals of Islam accordingly change their days of celebration and joy. The order of the months in the *Hijri* calendar is *Muharrum, Safar, Rabi-ul-Awwal, Rabi-ul-Sani, Jamadi-ul-Awwal, Jamadi-ul-Sani, Rajab, Shahban, Ramzan, Shawwal, Zi-Qad* and *Zil-Hijj*.

Festivals in India thus occur throughout the year due to diverse cultures and religions that follow their own calender. This book talks about the festivals of India in order of their occurrence, starting from the first month of the year - January, according to the Roman calendar.

LOHRI

Lohri is a seasonal harvest festival of northern India celebrated especially in the states of Punjab and Haryana. It is celebrated on the **13th of January** every year. In Punjab, wheat is the main winter crop, which is planted or sown in October and harvested in March or April. In January, the fields begin to show the promise of a good harvest and farmers celebrate Lohri before the cutting and gathering of crops! So Lohri means thanking the Gods for a good crop. Lohri is also about thanking the Sun God for bringing warmth. This time also signifies that after this day, the days start becoming longer and warmer and thus the chill of winter is on the decline.

Lohri is usually celebrated in the evenings. A huge bonfire is lit in the middle of a ground or open area in front of homes! What is the significance of a bonfire? It symbolizes the sun during the Lohri celebrations! Going around the fire is considered holy and is important before anyone joins the celebration! Seasonal savories and sweets like popcorn, *rewari*, *gajak*, peanuts and sugar cane are eaten. Every one prays and circles around the bon fire, throwing fistfuls of these sweets and savories.

After going around the bon fire, people meet friends and relatives, exchange greetings and gifts! They pick up the eatables tossed about the fire and distribute them as *prasaad* (holy offerings) to everyone. The men do their foot tapping *Bhangra* dance to the beat of the *dholak* and the women perform the more gentle *Gidda* dance! Everyone gets up to dance hearing the energetic beat of the drums! The first Lohri of a new bride or a newborn baby is celebrated with much more gaiety and fanfare. Everybody is invited to join the party and the dancing goes on till the wee hours of the morning. Favourite winter food like makki-ki-roti (multi-millet hand-rolled bread) and sarson-ka-saag (cooked mustard herbs) are eaten around the bonfire! Lohri is a fun filled festival of the fun-loving people of India.

Lohri Celebrations

The rice dish or pongal

Can you ever imagine a festival being named after a dish? Well, India with its rich and vibrant culture, has such a festival! On the **fourteenth of January** (the next day after Lohri), when there are newly harvested rice grains, a dish is prepared! Sesame seeds, jaggery, chickpeas, groundnuts and dried coconut are added to the rice grains. These ingredients are all put into a pot of milk and boiled until the milk spills over! This delicious 'dish' is called **'Pongal'**. *Pongal actually means* **boiled over!** Pongal is mostly prepared choosing an auspicious hour in the day. It is prepared in the courtyard of the house. This festival is popular in **South India** particularly in **Tamil Nadu** and **Andra Pradesh**.

Originally, Pongal was a harvest festival. In fact it falls on the same day as Makar Sankranti, a festival celebrated in North India. That is why it is called **Pongal Sankranti**. Pongal is a four day festival. On the **first day,** people pray to the **Rain God** (God Indra) and thank him. This is called **'Bhogi Pongal'**. This day is also related to the myth about *Lord Krishna* lifting the Mount Goverdhan on his little finger and protecting the people from the wrath of Indra, the rain God!

Women making Rangoli

Shiv ordering Nandi to live on earth

Useless articles of the house are thrown out into a fire made of wood and cow dung. Hymns are sung in the praise of God. *'Rangoli Kolam'* is decorated on clean ground by the front doors or courtyard. Rangoli is a way of decorations done to welcome the festival. Rangoli is done with a variety of coloured powder, rice powder and tumeric powder. Apart from various floral designs, words like "Pongalo Pongal" meaning 'welcome to Pongal' is drawn too.

The **second day** is dedicated to praying to **'Surya'** or **Sun God**. It is called **'Surya Pongal'**. In the morning, family members get together in the courtyards of their homes and **cook Pongal!** There is a chorus of "Pongal Pongal" when the pot boils over! People rejoice and pay obeisance to the Sun God too! The dish is then shared by family and friends. The overflowing rice in the pot signifies prosperity for the family.

It is on the **third day** of Pongal or **Mattu-Pongal** that the cow or the Gau-puja is done. One legend says that **Lord Shiv** asked his bull, Nandi, to go to earth and deliver a message. The message was to tell the people on earth to have an oil bath every day and eat food once a month.

Cow worship

But Nandi got all mixed up. He told the people that Lord Shiv had said to have an oil bath once a month and eat everyday! When Lord Shiv heard this, he was very displeased. He said that now people would need more grain to eat so as a punishment Nandi would return to earth and help plough fields and grow more grains!

Thus, on this day, cows are bathed and decorated. Their horns are cleaned and artistically painted. The cows are given Pongal to eat. *Aarti* (circulating of a prayer plate or *thali*) is performed to ward off the evil eye! Actually in ancient times, the amount of cattle signified the wealth of a family!

Jallikathu, an event, is held in some places of Tamil Nadu. In this event, ferocious bulls find their horns tied with bundles of money. Men tussle with

Jallikathu

the bulls trying to get back the bundles! The successful men become village heroes. That must be so exciting! There is feasting and festivity after that. Cattle are decorated and taken out in a procession amidst much fanfare! The **fourth day** is known as **Kaanum Pongal**. Family members visit each other on this day. Sisters pray for the welfare of their brothers. This is very similar to the festival of *Raksha Bandhan* in the North!

MAKAR SANKRANTI

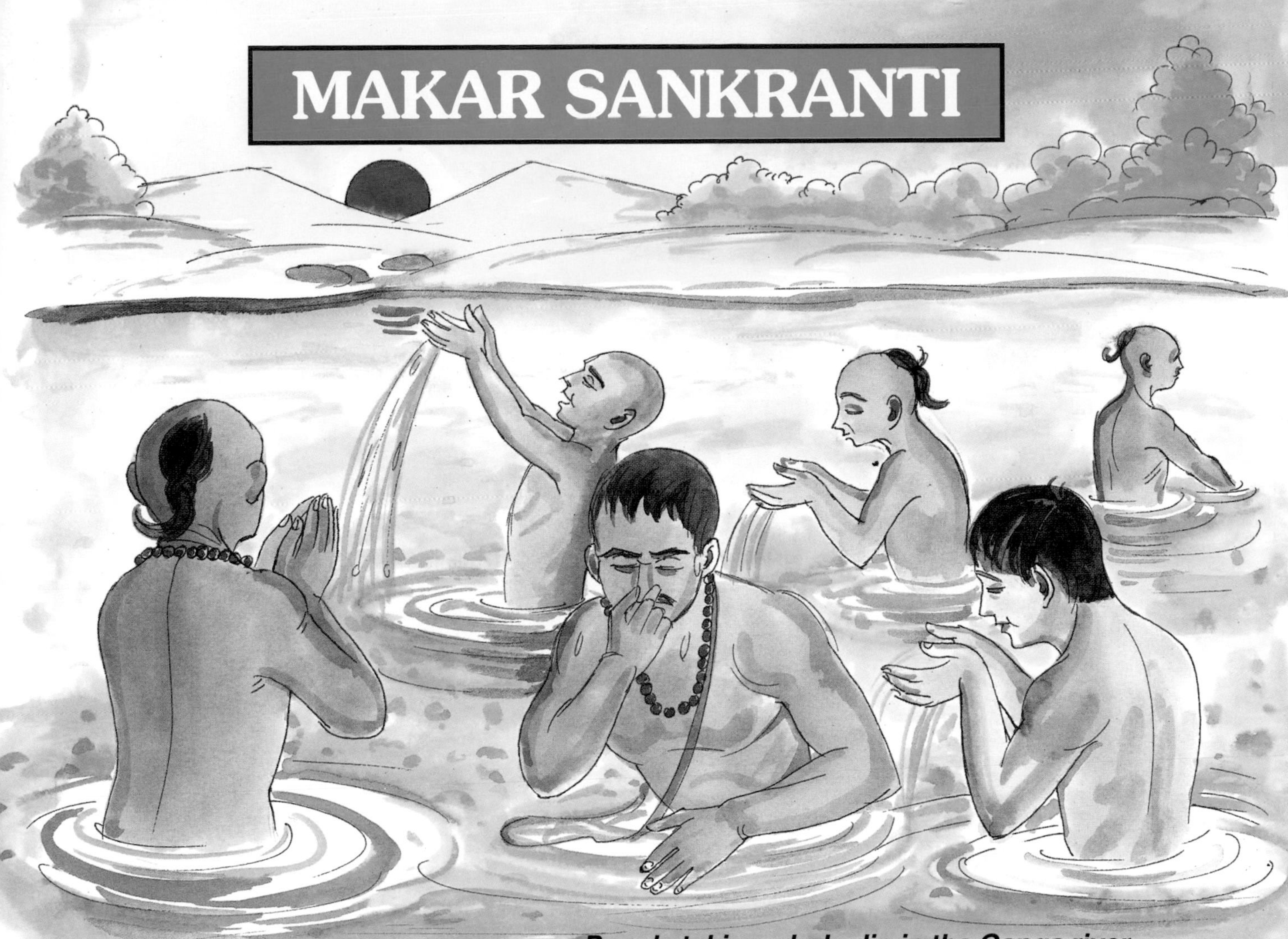

People taking a holy dip in the Ganga river

Makar Sankranti is an important Hindu festival celebrated on the **14th of January** every year, a day after the festival of Lohri! The date is fixed, unlike most of the other Indian festivals! The reason being that most Indian festivals are based on the lunar calendar. That means the day of the festival is decided on the movement of the moon. However, Sankranti is based on the solar or sun movements! This day symbolizes the start of the sun's journey to the northern hemisphere. This festival is the counterpart of Pongal, the popular festival of South India. On Makar Sankranti, it is traditional to take a dip in the holy Ganges and pray for our ancestors. The dip denotes washing away sins too! It is believed that the divine Goddess Ganga descended to earth during this time. How did Ganga descend on earth from her heavenly abode?

Sage Kapila turns his gaze towards the princes

This myth begins ages ago. King Sagar was performing the holy '*Ashvamedha Yagna*'. This *yagna* or holy prayer in front of a sacred fire is performed with a horse. A horse was set free to roam the world. If he came back unopposed, it meant victory for the king. The extent of territory the horse covered, would become the property of the king who had released him! Then, the returning horse was to be solemnly sacrificed to the Gods! A mishap occurred when King Sagar was carrying out this *yagna*! During the ceremony, his horse got lost! "Go and find the horse!" king Sagar instructed his 60,000 sons.

So his sons set out to search for the horse. Sadly, they could not find it! After a tiring search they reached the ashram of sage Kapila. And do you know what they saw there? None other than the lost horse! The 60,000 sons of King Sagar were livid.

"He has stolen this horse!" they decided amongst themselves. At that time, sage Kapila was in deep meditation. Marching up to the sage they bellowed, "Sage Kapila how dare you steal the horse of king Sagar!" The sage remained immobile. He was still in meditation, you see! The princes continued to speak very harsh, accusing words. Eventually disturbed and very angry, sage Kapila opened his eyes. Turning his burning gaze towards the accusing princes, he reduced them to ashes! 60,000 sons of king Sagar were reduced to ashes by the sage's blazing eyes!

Prince Bhagirath praying to Goddess Ganga

These ashes were then sent to the nether worlds. King Sagar was horrified when he learned about this tragedy. He immediately sent his grandson Anshuman to plead to the sage to undo the curse. Anshuman travelled to the nether worlds and begged the sage. "Great sage, I beg you to undo the curse you have put on the 60,000 sons of king Sagar!" said he earnestly. Impressed with his persistence, Kapila answered, "Son, there is only one solution!"

"What great sage!" Anshuman asked eagerly.

"They can only be brought back to life if they are washed with the holy waters from the river Ganga!"

When Anshuman told this to king Sagar, the king wailed, "But the river Ganga is in the heavens above! My sons lie here on earth! How can I possibly bring her here?" The task of bringing Ganga to earth failed miserably! King Sagar's kin could not bring her to earth.

After two generations, Prince Bhagirath lamented the fate of his ancestors. He explored ways and means to do something about it. On learning that their sins could only be washed away by the holy waters of Ganga, he prayed hard to the heavenly river.

"O mother Ganga, please help me in my hour of need!" Finally, Goddess Ganga agreed to descend on earth. "But if I descend on the young earth my impact will split it into two!" Ganga warned the prince. This time, prince Bhagirath prayed to Lord Shiv who agreed to help him.

"I will take the massive impact on my matted head. This way the rushing waters will lose their force. It will make it easier for a descent on earth!" declared Lord Shiv.

And that is what exactly happened! With Shiv's help, Ganga descended on earth. Bhagirath led the river Ganga towards the ashes of his ancestors. Ganga split into many rivers. Why did she do this? She was trying to find the exact spot where the ashes were lying. Ganga was able to wash away their sins and release them from the curse. After washing the ashes, she went into the sea. Do you know that even today a popular fair is held at the Sagar Island? This is the island where Ganga meets the Bay of Bengal. It is believed those who bathe at the union of the river and the sea on Makar Sankranti are blessed by the Gods!

It is also said that on the day of Makarsankranti, the sun begins to rise higher and higher towards the Northern Hemisphere. People believe that God is reminding everyone to go up towards more brightness and light, away from darkness! On Makar Sankranti, devotees bathe in the *Ganga* (Ganges) river before sunrise. They pray to the rising sun. They chant the **Gayatri Mantra**

Children flying kites

and offer flowers. They pray for a good and righteous life. They also offer water to their ancestors, asking for blessings. Charity to the needy in the form of rice and *dal* is distributed. People even plan a menu for eating simple 'kichari', (mish-mash of *dal* and rice). This is to shine importance on 'simple living and high thinking' theory. Jaggery laddoos dotted with sesame seeds are eaten. People rejoice the coming of the harvest season. Special prayers are offered as a thanksgiving for good harvest! People welcome the end of freezing winter months and the arrival of the warm, bright sun.

In Punjab, Makar Sankranti is called Lohri. It is celebrated to rejoice harvest. In Bengal, the huge Ganga Sagar Mela commences. In Gujarat, this is the time for kite flying! In Maharashtra, people exchange 'til' laddoos! In the south, it is called Pongal. However, whichever state this festival is in it focuses on the joys of bright happy thoughts! It prompts people to move away from dark negativity and thank God for all he has given.

BASANT PANCHAMI

Basant or 'Vasant' means the season of spring! This is the season where the farmers cheer seeing the fields dancing with mustard flowers! This is the time of bloom and growth! It falls on the fifth day of the *Magha Shukla Paksha* (February-March) according to the Hindu calendar. Basant Panchami festival is the first day of spring. The *Goddess of Knowledge,* **Goddess Saraswati** is worshipped on this day.

Brahma with Saraswati

It is said that once, the creator Lord Brahma, reviewed his own creation, the Earth. He was struck by the sadness prevalent in the atmosphere. The trees and the forests were all silent. The creator wanted to change all this. He took some water from his *kamandal* (pot) and sprinkled on the earth. As soon as he did this, there was a blinding flash or lightning. And lo behold, a Goddess appeared. She was playing a musical instrument, the *veena,* with two hands.

Children praying to Goddess Saraswati

In her other two hands she held a book and a garland. Lord Brahma named her **Saraswati**, meaning the possessor of all *rasas* and *kalas* (fine arts and ecstasy). Lord Brahma asked the Goddess to fill the earth with the colours of music, dance, art and above all, education. Basant Panchami celebrates the creation of Goddess Saraswati.

On this day, children and adults perform **Saraswati Puja** (worship of Goddess Saraswati). People pray fervently for wisdom and knowledge The Goddess bestows the gifts of education, dance, music and the arts on people.

In some places, farmers worship their ploughs and begin sowing again. Beans of white radish and *ber* or berry is eaten! People wear yellow clothes and even make delicacies in the yellow colour. This is the season of yellow mustard, you see! Married women, apart from wearing yellow clothes, also adorn their wrists with yellow bangles. Basant Panchami ushers in the spring season with music, dance and frolic.

MAHA SHIVRATRI

"It is I who is superior!" stormed **Lord Brahma,** the creator, floating on his swan in the skies. **Lord Vishnu** the preserver laughed and dismissed this claim, "You know, you are completely mistaken. It is I who is the superior between you and me!"

A heated argument ensued. It got so fierce that the celestial kingdom of the Gods shook with a war of words!

The other Gods were worried. They went to Lord Shiv, the destroyer. The trinity of Gods is formed by the three, Brahma, Vishnu and Shiv. The lesser Gods approached these three, when any problem arose. *But now two of the three were locked in a verbal battle*! "They are quarrelling about who is superior of the two! Please do something!" cried the Gods. Shiv assured them that he would solve the dispute.

Taking the form of an unending column of fire, Shiv appeared in the middle of the conflicting duo! Brahma and Vishnu jumped apart not recognizing who had come between them!

"Find the beginning and the end of this column and he shall be declared superior!" came the instructions from the fiery, swaying brilliant pillar of light. The two disputing God's looked up the pillar of fire but there was no top visible. They looked down and there was no bottom! They decided to take the challenge. Brahma flew upwards on his swan tracing the top of the column. Vishnu went into the earth tracking the end of the column. Thousands of miles and many years of travel later, neither Vishnu nor Brahma were successful in their pursuit. During his futile search Brahma came across a Ketaki flower. "I was at the top. Some one had laid me as an offering! I have fallen down!" Ketaki blinked.

Brahma with Ketaki flower

Picking up Ketaki, Brahma looked up but there was no top. He knew she was lying. But he decided to tell a small white lie himself! While returning, Brahma heard Vishnu confess that he had not found the end of the column. "I have!" announced Brahma. "This is Ketaki! She is my witness!"

Oh no, Brahmaji had let ego guide his decision!

Enraged Shiv caught his lie! Manifesting himself back to his true form he admonished Brahma. A very embarrassed Brahma admitted he was lying.

"No one shall pray to you! No one will offer Ketaki as a flower to the Gods. She lied and gave a false testimony!" This was the day Shiv first manifested himself in the form of a lingam and righted a situation! The day is celebrated as the festival of Maha Shivratri. Worshipping Shiv on this day is believed to redeem mankind and shower prosperity on the world.

Some legends also say that it is the day when Shiv and Parvati got married!

Another interesting legend talks about a tribal called Lubdhak who was a devotee of Shiv. One day, he could not find his way out of a forest. Darkness fell. It was an eerie moonless night! Praying and trying to find his way out he saw a tiger! With a mighty roar, the tiger lunged to attack him. Knowing that he could not outrun the tiger, Lubdhak scrambled up a tree. Scared and very aware of the growling tiger pacing below, he muttered "*Om Namah Shivai!*"

Lubdhak climbs up the tree

"What if I fall asleep and fall down?" Worried Lubdhak. "Oh I shall pluck leaves from this tree to keep myself awake. So the entire night he plucked leaves and mumbled "*Om Namah Shivai!*" When he climbed down in the morning there was no trace of a tiger but at the base of the tree was a Shiv Lingam. Around it lay scattered leaves! The leaves Lubdhak had thrown from his perch had softly fallen all over the Lingam. Unwittingly, Lubdhak had offered leaves to the Lingam for the entire night!

Since it was a moonless night and the presence of Shiv in the form of a Lingam was there, this day is celebrated as Maha Shivratri. It is like Shiv promises that he is there to protect his devotees through a moonless night! This also signifies protection through difficult times. Maha Shivratri is celebrated as a grand festival in the month of *Phalgun* (March), on the thirteenth and fourteenth day of the waning moon. Individuals fast and stay awake throughout the night praying to Shiva. The chanting of '*Om Namah Shivai*' rings the air. Shiv temples are beautifully decorated.

The fast is broken the next morning. Hymns are sung throughout the night in praise of Shiv. People believe that all their sins will be washed away if they pray with proper devotion to Shiv on Maha Shivratri!

According to one ancient legend, during the churning of the ocean, a deadly pot of poison was thrown up. This disturbed the Gods and demons because the poison was so venomous it could destroy the world and mankind! Shiv agreed to swallow this poison and save the world! The poison was so toxic that his throat went blue. He was given the name of '*Neel Kantha*' or the blue throated one! This event is believed to be celebrated as Maha Shivratri! The day Shiv saved the world!

ID-UL-ZUHA

Ali knelt and offered Namaaz at the Mosque. His friend **Abdul** bent too. Ali and Abdul belonged to the **Muslim** Faith. This faith or religion is called **Islam**. Islam is an Arabic word meaning 'submission' or surrender to God. God is called 'Allah' in Islam. A person who submits to *Allah* and follows the teachings of *Islam* is called a *Muslim*.

Ali and Abdul were very seriously praying. Later, when their *Namaaz* (the Muslim way of prayer that is performed facing the direction where the holy city of Mecca would be) finished; they collected near a square to exchange notes. Their conversation was punctuated with excited anticipation! Why were Abdul and Ali so keyed up? Well, today was the Muslim festival of **Bakr Id.** Bakr Id is also known as **Id-ul-Zuha**. It falls on the tenth day of the twelfth month, i.e. *Zil-Hijj of the Hijri calendar* (Islamic calendar).

Muslim children offering Namaz

"*Ammi* (mother) has prepared biryani that I cannot wait to eat!" Ali told Abdul.

"Oh, *Abbu* (father) and *Ammi* are taking me to meet *Chacha* and *Chachi jaan* (uncle and aunt) so my meal will have to wait!" Abdul replied.

"*Ammi* said we shall meet family and friends today! We will also distribute meat to the poor! You know what I mean no?" said Ali.

"Yes! My *Abbu* told me that one-third portion of the sacrificial animal meat is given to the poor, another third to relatives and the remaining for self and family. The sacrifice can be offered at any time before the afternoon!" Abdul explained very parrot like.

Abdul and Ali need not be reminded about why Id-ul-Zuha is such an important festival to all Muslims around the world! The festival is celebrated to mark the ordeals faced by **Prophet Ibrahim**, four thousand years ago, when he was following his true faith and belief in *Allah.*

What does *Prophet* mean? Islam says *Allah* resides in heaven with angels. Prophets or messengers are chosen by *Allah* to carry messages from Allah to the people on earth. Prophet Ibrahim is considered to be the father of prophets and also called one of the ancestors of the final **Prophet Muhammad**. According to legend, Prophet Ibrahim was put to a tough test to prove his loyalty to *Allah*. Prophet Ibrahim was very devoted to *Allah* and followed all his instructions with proper devotion. One day, Allah came in Ibrahim's dream telling him to sacrifice his son Ismail to show his loyalty to *Allah*. Without hesitation, both Ibrahim and Ismail agreed. But as Ibrahim was about to sacrifice his son, Allah switched Ismail with a **Ram** (male goat) at the last moment! Hence, on this day, Muslims offer sacrifices of a goat, sheep or camel all over the world. In India, a goat is usually offered for sacrifice.

Meat is partaken if the animal has been ritually slaughtered. It is then called *halal.* Thus, the message of Id-ul-Zuha is "get ready for sacrifice." Like the animal sacrifice, one should be ready to give up everything for common good. On this day, apart from prayers and performance of virtuous deeds, families and friends visit each other. Feasts are prepared and a festive atmosphere prevails!

City of Mecca

Children enjoying themselves on Id

Id-ul-Zuha also corresponds with the **Hajj pilgrimage to Mecca**. What is *Hajj*? Hajj is a pilgrimage made to the holy city of Mecca. It is believed Prophet Ibrahim faced many difficult tests when he was following his true faith. The city of Mecca has become a revered point of acknowledgment for all his tests. One visit to this city is a must for every Muslim. The Hajj to Mecca is a once-in-a-lifetime duty upon a Muslim male and female whose money or financial situation and health permit them to do so. Before going on the journey, a pilgrim should cleanse himself, pay his debts and still have enough money left for his journey and his family!

Muslim have to pray five times in the day in every time zone asking for *Allah's* blessing. When praying they should face the *Ka'bah*! What is the Ka'bah? This is a pillar devoted to the worship of one God in the holy city of Mecca. Even when away from the holy city of Mecca, a true Muslim prays in the direction where the city would be.

ID-MILAD-UN-NABI

Id-Milad-Un-Nabi is the day Prophet Muhammad was born. It was on the twelfth day of the third month of the Muslim year. Prophet Muhammad's death anniversary also falls on the same day. Prophet Muhammad is believed to be the last messengers from Allah - the Final Prophet. **Islam** was the name given to the religion preached by Adam, Ibrahim, and then Muhammad. Three months before Prophet Muhammad died, he had pronounced that Islam was complete. The main beliefs of the religion were compiled into the holy book named **'Quran'**.

On Id I Milad sermons are delivered in mosques. Eulogies sing praise of the Prophet. The life and deeds of Prophet Muhammad are addressed. The entire day is devoted to prayer. Alms giving is also a part of observing the importance of this day. Sweets are distributed and shared amongst everybody.

HOLI

"Bura na mano HOLI Hai! (Do not mind, today is Holi!)" is a cry that resonates many lanes and alleys, when India celebrates the festival of colour or Holi!

Holi is a festival that welcomes the bright and the colourful spring season. It is also a full-moon day and is celebrated in the month of *Phalgun* (February-March) of the Hindu Lunar calendar. A fun filled festival for people of all ages. Bonfires blaze and everyone paints colours on each other!

Houses are spring- cleaned and mouth slurping sweet meats and savories are made!

Why do we celebrate Holi? There are many legends and tales attached to this festival. Let me begin with the story of Lord Krishna. *Putna*, the she-demon, was sent by Lord Krishna's royal uncle Kansa to kill him. Putna pretending to feed him, took baby Krishna into her arms. But Krishna saved himself by killing her first! Her death is celebrated as Holi! It seems she represents winter and her death means spring arriving with a merry step!

But this is not the only story attached to the reasons for celebrating Holi! There is another tale. It says that young Krishna would complain to his mother Yashoda about why Radha was so fair and he so dark. Yashoda advised him to smear colour on Radha's face and see her colour change too! So that's what he did and ever since we enjoy the festival of colours!

Lord Krishna was very naughty and loved playing pranks on the village belles. One prank saw him throw coloured powder over them! That started a yearly ritual called Holi!

Krishna and Putna

Krishna playing with colours

One of the most popular legends explaining why we celebrate Holi is the story of Prahlad. It is said that the demon-king Hiranyakashyapu's son Prahlad was an ardent follower of Vishnu. This upset the king because he wanted everyone to regard him and only him as God! But, Prahalad refused to accept his father as God because he believed only in Lord Vishnu. This enraged the king and he decided to kill his own son!

Prahlad with Holika

Hiranyakashyapu commanded his sister Holika to carry Prahlad in her arms and walk into burning flames. Holika would be saved because she had a boon from the God of flames and the lad in her arms would die. But, exactly the opposite happened. Lord Vishnu saved the lad and Holika died. How did this happen?

Narsingha kills Hiranyakashyapu

Hiranyakashyapu did not know that for one hour in the day, the boon or protection from flames did not work. Unfortunately for Holika, the time chosen to enter the flames and kill the lad fell at the same hour! When the flames leapt up, Holika died as the boon did not work and Prahlad was saved by Lord Vishnu. Later Lord Vishnu took the *avtaar* (form) of *Narsingha* (half man and half lion) and killed Hiranyakashyapu. That is why a night before Holi, bonfires are lit depicting this very tale!

The next day of Holi is 'rang' meaning colour. The revelry is fabulous. The houses are cleaned. Dirt and junk are swept out. Some people burn junk and get rid of bacteria too! In fact, Holi fire is a symbol of destruction of all rubbish and contamination! Holi also means 'sacrifice'. Burn all the impurities of the mind such as egoism vanity, etc., through the fire of devotion and knowledge.

In some states, Holi is riotous fun. People organize water fights. You know how we have mock brawls with spray guns and toy water pistols. Everyone is cannoned by splashing water! Also, balloons filled with water target many innocent passing pedestrians or cars, accompanied by the cry, *"Bura na manoo Holi hai! (Don't get upset, it's Holi)"* Groups dance and sing at the beat of the *dholak* or drums. People even consider this to be the best time to bury old fights and become friends again! During Holi, most folks prefer to wear white clothes so the colours show up more! Children love this festival as they can

Delicacies of Holi

No festivity is complete without the festival food. During Holi, we eat *gujiya* (a sweet pastry filled with *khoya*) then home made potato chips, rice crisps, *papads* (papadams) and *chakli* (sweet meat)!

Sadly, Holi is becoming pretty boisterous and sometimes irritating. People are misusing this fun time. Instead of healthy powdered colours, they throw eggs, paints, chemical dyes and sometimes tar! On the other hand, some mischievous elements even take this opportunity to forcibly colour and trouble people because it is Holi! This is so wrong and each one of us should make it point to rebuff this kind of abuse on a festival meant to be pure and merry!

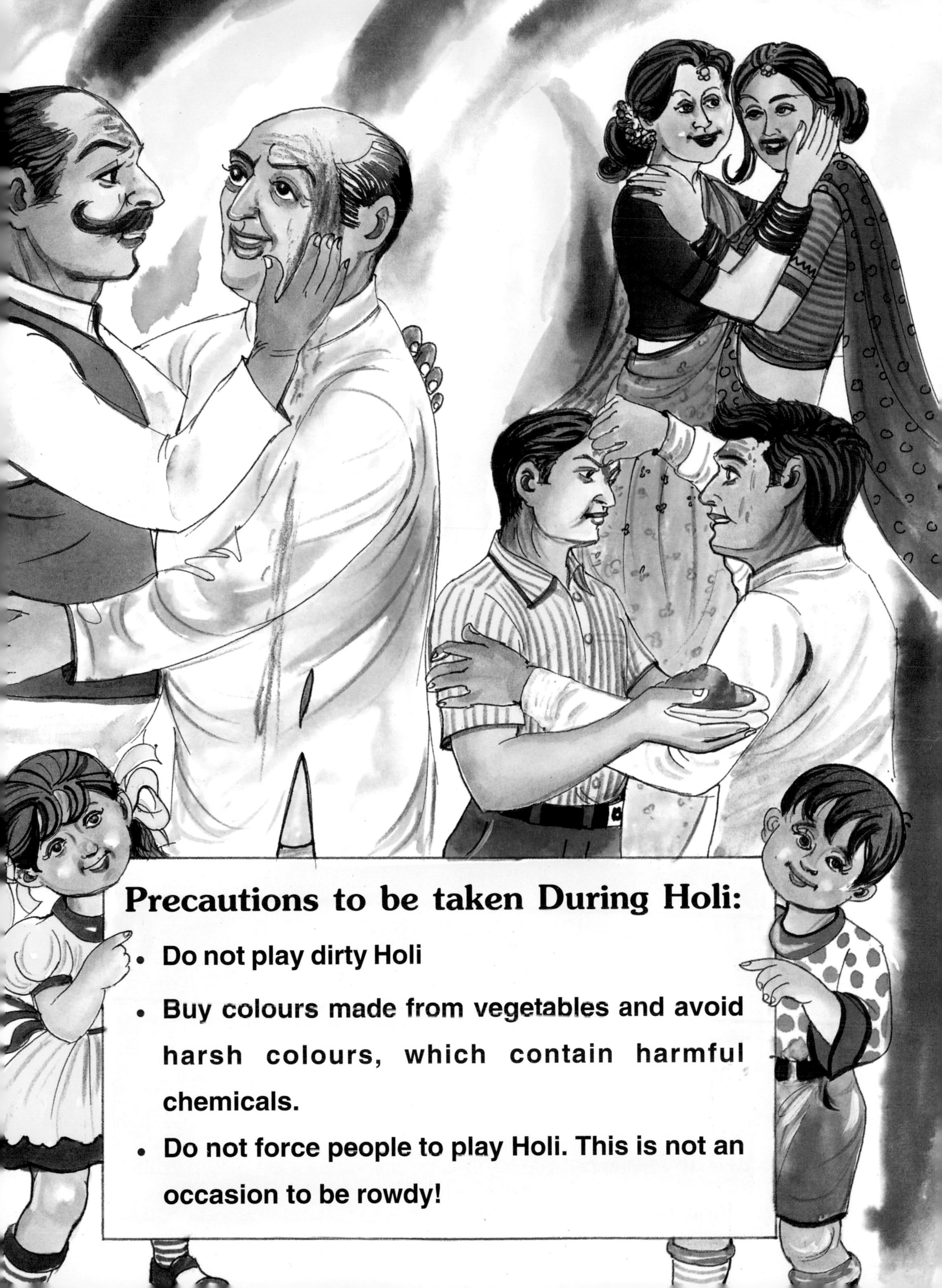

Precautions to be taken During Holi:

- Do not play dirty Holi
- Buy colours made from vegetables and avoid harsh colours, which contain harmful chemicals.
- Do not force people to play Holi. This is not an occasion to be rowdy!

PURIM AND PESAH

Purim is a **Jewish festival** celebrated in **March**. This festival is celebrated to rejoice the escape of the Jews from the clutches of the Persian king. It is believed that the king wanted to kill all the Jews. But the king's wife, the queen, who was a Jew herself, saved her people even at the cost of risking her own life.

On the day of Purim, the story of how the Jews escaped is read. In the evening, the whole family gets together with friends for a feast. Gifts are exchanged. Charity is also distributed. It is traditional to give at least two poor people some sort of monetary help on this day.

Purim is followed by another important Jewish festival known as the **Pesah** or passover. It is celebrated in mid April over a period of eight days. Why do Jews celebrate Pesah? This festival marks the 'passing over' or sparing of the Jews by the Angel of Death in 1250 B.C! It is said that when Jewish families were sad and wanted to leave Egypt, to escape the massacre, Moses instructed them to mark their doorway with blood.

At night, when the Angel of Death visited Egypt, she passed over the Jewish households and spared the Jewish children. The next day, when the *Pharaoh* (Egyptian king), let the Jews leave Egypt, they simply fled without any delay. Moses successfully led them out. Jews believe that the divine lord helped Moses guide the enslaved Jews out of Egypt to the Promised Land, now called Israel.

Unleavened bread is considered sacred on this day. When Jews left Egypt, they did not wait to bake bread. They just carried the dough. After praying, they took out the unleavened bread and everyone ate it. This bread is known as *Matzah. The* festival is a family festival and is celebrated in the homes. Homes are made sparkling clean for the festival.

Moses leading the Jews

RAM NAVAMI

King Dashrath with lord Agni

King Dashrath was childless. His kingdom of Ayodhya was at a height of prosperity but there were no heirs to inherit it! He had three wives, Kaushalya, Kaikeyi and Sumitra; but no children.

In another part of the world, the king of Lanka, **Ravan**, was terrorizing his subjects! Through severe penance, Ravan had taken a boon from Brahma. The boon said that Ravan could never be killed by any heavenly being, may it be gods or demons! Hearing about his wickedness and arrogance, Brahma declared Ravan would be killed at the hands of man! The Gods who Ravan was troubling begged Vishnu to take charge and destroy Ravan. Vishnu agreed and decided to take birth as a human on earth.

King Dashrath performed a *yagna* in order to seek the blessings of the Gods, for a son. Pleased with king Dashrath's *yagna,* Lord Agni arose from the sacred fire.

He gave a bowl of *kheer* to the king and asked him to distribute it amongst his queens. After the queens consumed the *kheer*, in due course of time, a son was born to king Dashrath and queen Kaushalya. His son was called **Ram** and is supposed to be the incarnation of lord Vishnu. Yes, Lord Vishnu came to earth born as Ram! Prince Ram grew to be what people call a perfect human being. He was righteous, virtuous, fair and pure. Ram fulfilled his destiny with ease and killed Ravan, thus ridding the world of terror and fear. **Ramnavami** is a festival celebrated to **honour the birth of Ram**. It is celebrated on the ninth day of the *Shukla Paksha* in the month of *Chaitra* (April). On Ramnavami, devotees do *puja* (worship) of Lord Ram and sing devotional songs. People also observe a fast and only retain a light diet of fruits, milk and curds. It is believed that all toxins of the body are flushed out by this meal which is light and non spicy. Once you are purified from within, your devotion and worship to the divine will be more concentrated. The temples at home as well as outside are cleaned. Offerings of flowers and sweetmeats are made to the idols of Ram, his wife Sita and brother Laxman. There are public gatherings where hymns and songs in praise of Lord Ram are organized. In Ayodhya, the birth place of Lord Ram, it is celebrated with a special joy.

People praying to lord Ram

MAHAVIR JAYANTI

Lord Mahavir, the founder of Jainism

Mahavir Jayanti is celebrated to honour the birthday of **Lord Mahavir**, the founder of **Jain religion**. It is celebrated on the 13th day of the bright half of the *Chaitra* month, which falls usually during **March/April**. *Jainism* has twenty-four religious *Tirthankara* or the lords to guide the devotees in the world. Thirthankars are born as humans. Through spirituality and self-realization they reach a state of perfection and attain the status of God. They are considered to be Gods by the Jain community. Mahavir is considered to be the twenty-fourth and the last *Tirthankara* and was known as *jina* (meaning the conqueror of soul).

Mahavir was born in 599 B.C. to Siddhartha of Kundanpur and the Lichhavi princess Trisala. Before Mahavir was born, his mother had many dreams. These dreams showed auspicious signs and announced the coming of a very special baby. When she told her husband about the dreams, he told her that the baby was a *Tirthankar.* So you see, Mahavir was identified as a *Tirthankar* even before he was born!

Statue of Mahavir

Mahavir was fearless and always spoke the truth. He was genuinely concerned about the welfare of people. At the age of thirty, Prince Mahavir left his home and wandered seeking the truth about life and existence. He gave up every possession he owned, even the clothes covering his body. He undertook penance to find knowledge. Then, one day, after meditating and fasting for two and a half days under an Ashoka tree, Mahavir gained enlightenment.

The *Digambara* sect of Jains believe that during and after enlightenment Mahavir wore no clothes.

However, the *Svetambara* sect of Jainism believe that after gaining enlightenment Mahavir wore no worldly materials or clothes. However, it was Lord Indra who covered him with a white cloth afterwards. So the Digambara *sadhus* wear no clothes. They have renounced all worldly possessions. The Svetambara wear a pristine white cloth like shawl. Mahavir preached *ahinsa* (non-violence) and shunned worldly possessions.

Jain Temple

He preached that all souls were alike and humans corrupted their souls on their own. He said that one should not harm anybody, not even an insect, as every living being had a consciousness. He also believed God was omnipresent. Lord Mahavir also discouraged hoarding of excess wealth as it brings misery and strife. He preached the three *Ratnas*, namely right conduct, right knowledge and right faith.

On **Mahavir Jayanti**, the followers of Jainism visit the Jain temples and chant prayers. They offer flowers in the temple. Images of Mahavir are taken out in a chariot amidst a huge procession. The procession finishes its journey at a temple or a large ground set aside for this purpose. Many devotees participate in the procession. Donations in the form of clothes, food and even medicines are distributed on this day. Sermons are told and scriptures are chanted. Since Rajasthan and Gujarat have a larger Jain population, this festival holds more significance there. However, it is celebrated by Jains all over the world and is a big day for them.

BAISAKHI

Guru Gobind Singh with his followers

Baisakhi is always celebrated on a fixed date according to the solar calendar, on the **13th of April**. In Punjab, this festival is celebrated with great fanfare. It is one of the main festivals of the Sikhs. In fact, Sikhs all over the world venerate this festival with enthusiasm.

Guru Nanak Dev was the founder and the first Guru of the Sikh religion. After him there were nine more Gurus. On the Baisakhi day, in the year 1699, Guru Gobind Singh, the tenth and the last Guru, laid the foundation of the *Khalsa Panth* or the path of the pure. He wanted the Sikhs to be valiant, daring and protective of their religion and of peace. He called his followers to Anandpur and asked them to give a test of fearlessness.

The Guru asked one of the daring disciples to go with him in the tent. He then came out with a blood-soaked sword. In the same way, he took four more disciples inside the tent who remained undaunted by his act. Later, when they all returned safe and sound, he declared them his 'Panj Pyare', meaning five favourites.

Then, he asked his followers to maintain certain principles to become a pure Sikh. The last names of the five were replaced by the suffix 'Singh' meaning lion. This was to apply for all the Sikhs there on. The ladies names were suffixed by 'Kaur', meaning Lioness. By this move all caste barriers were removed! Guru Gobind Singh declared the five emblems of the Sikhs at this meeting. They were the five 'K's. These were: **Kesh** (uncut hair), **Kangha** (comb), **Kara** (a metal wristband), **Kirpan** (sword) and **Kachha** (undergarment shorts). These five symbols were to become the identity of being a true 'Khalsa' Sikh.

He instructed Sikhs to greet each other by saying, *'Wahe guru ji ka Khalsa, Wahe guru ji ki Fateh'* meaning '*Khalsa* belongs to God and to God alone belongs the victory.' He gave a call to the Sikhs to unite and fight against the harassment by the Mughal rulers in those days. On this auspicious day, the **Guru Granth Sahib** was declared as the eternal Guru of the Sikhs and all followers of Sikhism were to revere it.

On Baisakhi, people flock to *Gurudwaras* (Sikh worship places) and listen to the recitations of the **Guru Granth Sahib**. The Golden Temple in Amritsar draws huge crowds on this day. It is very auspicious to take a dip in the lake surrounding the Golden Temple too. On this day, *langars* or free community meals happen at the *Gurudwaras*. Everyone helps to make a *langar* a success. So, while some clean the *Gurudwara*, others serve the meals or cook in the kitchens. Special cuisine is made to mark the occasion. The *Gurudwaras* are illuminated on this day, which is also regarded as the New Year's day.

At this harvest festival, celebrations are held in the countryside and community dancing takes place with much gaiety and gusto. People dress in their typical folk dance clothes and the men perform the *Bhangra* dance while the women do the *Gidda* folk dance. The drums or *dholak* play incessantly and the beat and tunes synchronize with every dance step!

Men performing the Bhangra

Is Baisakhi celebrated all over India or in Punjab only? Baisakhi is celebrated in other parts of the nation under different names. In Kerala, the festival is called **Vishu** and is celebrated as the New Year's day. People exchange gifts and greetings. In the state of Andhra Pradesh, it is celebrated as **Ugadi** or the new beginning. Traditionally, a nutritious chutney is made from new neem flowers, green mangoes and jaggery. In Bengal, it is known as **Naba Barsha**, meaning New Year. In Manipur, it is known as **Lai Haraoba** when people sing and dance. Assamese celebrate the festival as **Bohag Bihu**, and the community arranges feasts, music, and dancing! In Maharashtra, it is known as the **Gudi Padva** in which new clothes and festive food add to the spirit of fun and celebrations. Thus, in the month of April, the days thirteenth to fifteenth are very special days of festivities in various parts of the country.

EASTER

Easter is celebrated on the Sunday after the full moon in the month of **April**. It recalls the Resurrection of Jesus Christ. It is a day of great joy for the followers of **Christianity.** Christians believe Lord Jesus descended on earth from the heavens to remind people about God and leave the paths of wicked ways. Jesus was called the Son of God. Jesus performed many miracles and drew people towards his sermons. Alas! He made many enemies and the ruling priests of that era had him arrested without a fair trial. He was sentenced to death. His sentence was that he would be nailed to a cross and left to die. To the sorrow of his disciples, he was suffering tremendously. In-spite of so much suffering, he kept asking God to forgive his tormentors. Jesus muttered, "Forgive them Lord, for they do not know what they are doing!" After Jesus died, two of his disciples brought his body down from the cross and placed him in a tomb.

Jesus Christ

Jesus returns from the dead

A miracle occurred after three days! *Jesus returned from the dead!* The day Lord Jesus died on the cross is called **Good Friday**. It is a day for mourning, sermons, prayers and fast. People go to the church for the ceremony. It is believed that since Lord Christ died for the good of mankind, this day is particularly holy. Hence the name Good Friday.

After three days comes Easter Sunday! A festival of joy on Christ's return! People exchange cards and Easter eggs, that being a symbol of Jesus' return and new life to Christians! The humble egg assumes importance on Easter because it signifies the beginning of a new life. The most popular tradition is of decorating Eggs on Easter. Children paint Easter eggs in different patterns and give them as gifts. The traditional way to celebrate Easter is to visit graves of departed souls. People go to churches and sing hymns and offer prayers. The flame from a candle lighted by the priest is used to light other candles, symbolizing the spread of light and goodwill in mankind on Easter. People exchange good wishes amongst themselves on this day.

Easter Bunny symbolizes the coming of spring and life. Some games are also played. Easter Bunny is supposed to have hidden the Eggs when the children were sleeping! Of course parents and elder siblings are the actual 'Easter Bunnies', but we are not going to tell are we? The child who finds the most eggs gets a prize! Children have fun locating eggs supposedly hidden by the Easter Bunny around the house!

Then there is the game of Egg Roll! No it is not an eatable! Here you have to roll the egg on grassy slopes to great distances. The idea is not to break the egg! On Easter, you get to taste delicious egg shaped chocolates. In fact, confectionery shops are filled with innovative egg shaped chocolates, candies and cakes!

BUDDHA PURNIMA

Siddharth sees the 'four sights'

Once upon a time, there lived a prince named Siddharth. He was born on a full moon day in the year 544 B.C. at Lumbini in Nepal. His father was king Shuddhodana, the mighty ruler of Kapilavastu. On his birth, the astrologers had declared, "This is a very exceptional child. He will either become a great king or abandon house and home to become a monk." This prediction made the king worried as he thought that he might lose his precious son. So, he tried his level best to make him attached to earthly objects and keep him away from the miseries of life. It is said that he had three palaces for three seasons built for his son. The little prince had everything he wanted. Siddharth was living in the lap of luxuries and should have been the happiest person on earth. But he was not! He was restless and sad. His heart appeared troubled and uneasy. Later, Siddharth got married to princess Yashodhara and they had a son named Rahul.

One day, prince Siddharth went around the city in his chariot, driven by his old faithful servant Channa. There he saw four sights which changed his entire life. He saw an old man, a sick man, a dead man and an ascetic. Channa told him that everybody on this earth has to pass through the first three stages in their life span. Siddharth became very upset on hearing this. He could not understand why there was so much of pain and suffering everywhere. He began to question the very existence of human beings if they have to die one day.

One night, overcome with his unanswered questions, Siddharth left his son and sleeping wife in the opulent palace and went into the world seeking answers. He wandered around for many years. Then, one day, while meditating under a peepal tree, a brilliant light awakened his soul and he understood the answers to every question, which had been worrying his soul for so long!

Siddharth was now *Buddha, the Enlightened one*. Common people gathered about him to listen to what he had to say because he spoke their language. He spread the message of non-violence and peace. He said that too much of attachment to worldly goods led to sin. "Lead a life of honesty and commitment!" Buddha told his followers. He believed that everyone's rebirth depended on ones own conduct. Even though suffering was inevitable, the degree of suffering could be controlled by one's own behaviour. That means if you do good deeds, surely the rewards would lead to a better life. Likewise if your deeds are bad then you shall be punished with more suffering.

The birth anniversary of Buddha is celebrated as **Buddha Purnima.** It falls on the full moon day in the month of *Baisakh* (April-May). This is considered a very holy day for Buddhists. Buddhists are the followers of Buddhism or the religion preached by Buddha. Buddhists bathe and wear white clothes on Buddha Purnima or Jayanti. They offer prayers at their monasteries or places of worship. Special attention is paid to peepal trees. That is because it was under a peepal tree that Buddha attained enlightenment. Diyas and lamps are lit around the trees. Weeds are rooted out and the trees are decorated with flowers. Devotees also place bright flags. In their prayers, they promise to follow the 'panchsheel principles' (five principles) told by Buddha. These principles are -(1) Do not steal (2) Do not lie (3) Do not drink intoxicant liquor (4) Do not take any living being's life (5) Do not commit adultery.

Kaza festival

Devotees place fruits under the trees too. Charity in the form of food, clothes and alms are also distributed. As a symbol of freedom, caged birds are freed on Buddha Purnima. Celebrations are very festive in Bodhgaya in Bihar and in Sarnath in Uttar Pradesh. Also places like Arunachal Pradesh, Sikkim and Ladakh, where there is a large Buddhist population, this festival is celebrated with zest.

Another important Buddhist celebration is the **Kaza Festival** of Ladakh held in the month of June. Here the Dalai Lama is worshipped as the living incarnation of Lord Buddha. People do a mask dance on this day to frighten away evil spirits.

PATETI

Fire worship

Pateti is a **Parsi** festival. This festival marks the beginning of the New Year for the Parsis. Parsis belong to the ancient **Zoroastrian** religion. Zoroastrianism is a faith founded by Zoroaster in ancient Persia. In this faith, fire is worshipped as the son of *Ahura Mazda*, the representative of God. The holy place of worship of the Parsis is the fire temple known as *agiary.* Parsis believe that Zoroaster brought the sacred fire from heaven to earth. This fire is kept burning by the high priest of the agiary. This religion's main tenets are about the struggle between the good and the evil. Zoroastrians believe gladness is a weapon to swathe and cut away evilness! Their belief is in purity. Fire, water and earth should be carefully kept pure by one and all!

The Pateti day brings joy and festivities for the Parsis. The majority of Parsis wear traditional new clothes consisting of sacred vests, *gara sarees, duglees* and ornaments. Then, the Parsi family goes to the fire temple or *agiary.* People pray and repent over their sins. They make resolutions to keep a pure mind and soul. They offer milk, flowers, water, fruits and even sandalwood to the sacred fire. The house is also decorated with flowers and rangolis, in which the motif of a fish is used. On Pateti day, feasting on Parsi delicacies like dhan, daal, fish, chicken, mutton and a variety of desserts is initiated. Another important aspect of Pateti is charity and Parsis distribute sweets and food to the poor. The day on which Pateti falls is noteworthy since it falls on the spring equinox, that is, the day and the night are of equal duration and both the North Pole and the South Pole have sunlight!

Another important day for the Parsis is **Khordad Sal.** It is the birthday of their prophet Zoroaster. Khordad Sal comes six days after Pateti. On this day, special prayers and discourses are held in the *agiary* on good deeds, good thoughts and charity.

RATH YATRA

Imagine a chariot which is made of *neem* wood, is yellow in colour and 14 metre high with 16 wheels. Each wheel measures seven feet in diameter and the chariot is pulled by 4,200 devotees! Who could be riding this magnificent chariot? **Lord Jagannath** of course!

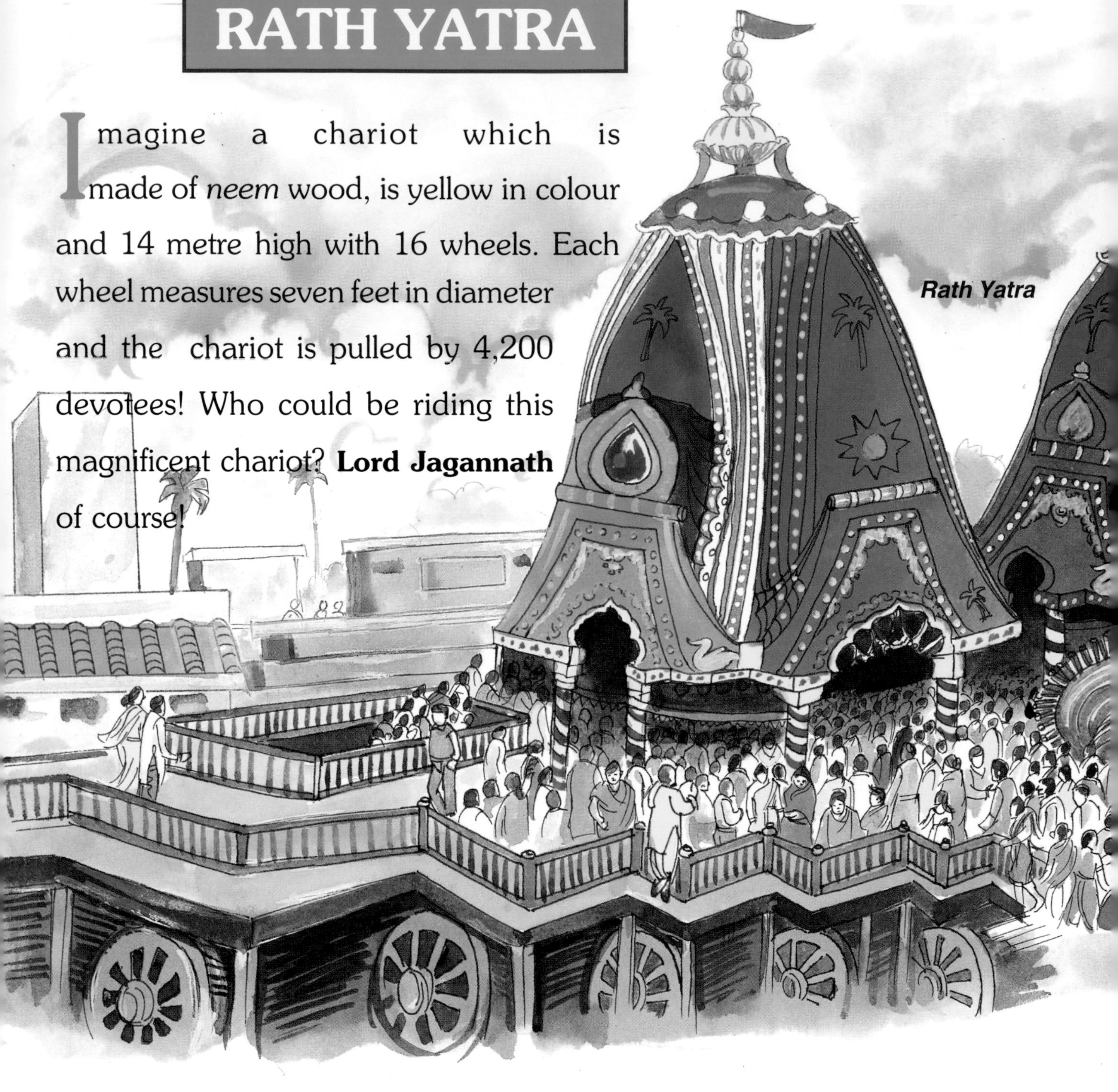

Rath Yatra

This chariot signifies the celebration of a unique festival, **Rath Yatra**. As the name suggests, Rath Yatra indicates a 'chariot ride'. The event is in honour of Lord Jagannath, another name of Lord Krishna. It is celebrated especially in the state of Orissa in the month of *Aashadh* (June-July). Even though this festival is celebrated in other places too, the main Rath Yatra takes place in the holy town of Puri at Orrisa.

The magnificent Jagannath temple in Puri celebrates the 'Rath' or chariot 'Yatra' or journey with pageantry and festive mood! A procession inaugurates at the Jagannath Temple annually around the months of June and July.

Lakhs of people visit Puri to witness this experience! In the Jagannath temple, Lord Krishna, his elder brother Balrama and their sister Subhadra are worshipped in an unusual trinity. Their images are made of *neemwood* and are painted in a highly stylised method.

But, why is the idol housed in the temple incomplete? Legends say that they were incomplete because their creator Vishwakarma was disturbed by a curious king. The craftsman was so angry that he refused to complete the statue. But the king decided to install the statue anyhow. That is why even today an incomplete idol is worshipped at the Jagannath temple!

What is the origin of the Rath Yatra? No one really knows. One reason given is that a chariot was drawn to transport the imperfect statue to the constructed temple. Since the first journey was made in a chariot this became a part of the custom. According to the other legends, Subhadra wanted to visit Dwarka, her parents home. Therefore, her two brothers Jagannath and Balabhadra took her there on this day. One legend says that Lord Jagannath is said to have voiced his longing to visit his birthplace Gundicha Ghar once yearly. That was the beginning of the *Yatra*. Whichever the legends are, the journey is made in elaborate chariots amidst fervent devotion by lakhs of people! Lord Jagannath, Lord Balabadhra and Subadhra travel in separate chariots. Lord Jagannath rides a 14 metre high chariot with sixteen wheels. Lord Balabadhra also rides a similar blue chariot with fourteen wheels and Subhadra rides a twelve metre high, twelve wheeled chariot. Each chariot resembles the temple at Puri! The journey of the deities in the town of Puri begins at the Jagannath temple and ends at *Gundicha Ghar* or Lord Jaggannath's birthplace, now a temple 3 kms away.

People worshiping neem wood images of Krishna, Balram and Subhadra

Thousands of devotees pull these chariots by huge ropes to *Gundicha Mandir.* It is believed that whosoever pulls the chariot achieves *moksha* or salvation and if somebody unfortunately comes under the wheels, they too experience a life after death full of peace.

The day of the *yatra* resounds with the sounds of gongs, conch shells, trumpets and holy chants! The crowds are overcome with frenzy. Balabhadra, the eldest brother rides first, followed by Subhadra and then Lord Jagannath. This arduous uphill and downhill track takes almost ten hours to reach its destination.

After nine days, the idols are taken back to the Jagannath Temple in an identical parade. The city of Puri is dressed up for this day. A holiday is declared. Special sweet meats are made and distributed. Children make or buy miniature chariots and imitate the 'Rath Yatra by pulling the miniatures through the streets playfully!

TEEJ

Worship of Goddess Parvati

The lands are dry and arid. A consistent watch is kept on the skies. When will it come? What is every one waiting for? The rains of course!

Teej is a seasonal festival heralding the onset of the monsoon season in northern India. Teej symbolizes the coming of the monsoons! It is celebrated with much joy in the states of Rajasthan, Bihar, Uttar pradesh, Uttranchal and Delhi. Teej falls on the third day of the waxing moon in the month of *Shravan* (July-August).

The Teej festival is basically a women festival. It is about rejoicing Goddess Parvati's marriage with Lord Shiv. Married women pray to Shiv and Parvati to give them a long and successful married life. With the first drops of rain on the parched ground, festivities explode with pomp and show! Flower decorated swings are hung on trees. Women flashing colourful clothes and jangling bangles sing and swing. They also thank the rain Gods for rain.

Women pamper themselves at this time. Hands beautifully designed with 'mehendi' or 'henna' are flashed about. Women follow the tradition of dancing the '*dandiya*' dance. This dance is performed by, twirling, whirling women wielding sticks or 'dandiyas' in unison to the beat of tunes! Married girls go to their mother's house for feast and fun and get gifts from their parents. This is the time when girls who are engaged receive gifts from their future in laws. A special sweet called 'ghewar' is eaten too! Many Teej *melas* or fairs are also organised all over where stalls of bangles, clothes and eatables are very popular.

RAKSHA BANDHAN

Ten years old Mala rested her chin on her knee and let out a deep sigh. Mala was very anxious today. Tomorrow was the festival of **Raksha Bandhan** and she wanted to give a special '*raakhi*' or sacred thread to her brother Om. Sadly, they were so poor that it was impossible to buy the fancy raakhis displayed in colourful rows all over the *bazaars*. She looked at the simple silk thread she had bought and let out another sigh.

"Why are you so sad *beti* (daughter)? asked her father, who was a labourer at a construction site.

"Father, It is not fair! I do not have enough money to buy a *raakhi* for bhaiya!" Tweaking her nose and smiling in an amused way, he sat next to her. They sat for some time. Suddenly, the street light on the pole ahead switched on, dispelling the gloom a little.

Mala, tying a *raakhi* is not about fancy threads! It is a never ending bond between a brother and sister! The thread is a witness of the lasting promise of

love between the two!" Mala turned to gaze at her father.

Her father looked at her and said gently "Do you know the significance of *Raksha Bandhan*?"

Mala shook her head saying "No."

Her father explained, "Nobody knows the origin of this festival. But some popular tales say that once **lord Indra** was in a war with the demons. The demons seemed to be winning and that was not good news for the Gods. Indra's wife decided to do something about it. She read some scriptures and chanted a holy mantra on a thread. She tied the thread on her husband's wrist telling him it was a '*Raksha Sutra*' or **protection thread**.

Indra went on to win the war and defeat the demons!"

"Really?" Mala exclaimed. "But father, how do you know all this?"

"My grandmother was an expert story teller!" father said laughing.

"She also told me that once long ago, the **Queen of Mewar** was being threatened by the mighty army of the Governor Bahadur Shah. He laid a siege around her kingdom. Well, the Maharani sent a sacred thread or *rakhi* to the **Mughal emperor Humayun**. On receiving it, Humayun felt he needed to protect his sister!"

"Why?" asked Mala.

"Such was the strength of the bond created by the thread! Humayun came to the queen's rescue and chased Bahadur Shah's army out!"

"Wow!" Mala chuckled.

Humayun receives a Rakhi from the Queen of Mewar

A sister tying Rakhi to protect brother in battle

"They say that in olden days, wars were so frequent that sisters tied this thread to protect their brothers in battles so that they would come back safe!"

Mala's mood lifted tremendously. "Father," she said, "a simple thread can signify a strong bond between brother and sister. Then, there is no need for fancy threads!"

Father tousled her hair and quipped, "Come, let us go in. You have to sleep early! Tomorrow is *Raksha Bandhan* !"

Over the years, *Raksha Bandhan* has become a very popular festival in India. It is celebrated as a festival signifying a loving bond between a brother and a sister. Raksha Bandhan falls on the full moon day in the month of *Shravan* (July-August).

The day begins with a bath. The brother sits on a wooden stool. His sister decorates a '*thali*' or plate with the sacred thread, tikka made of turmeric and vermillion, and some '*mithai*' or sweet delicacy. She ties the thread praying for her brother's health and prosperity. Her brother in turn makes a promise to protect her throughout his life and gives her a gift or some money!

Usually, this festival is between real brothers and sisters but over time cousins too regard the tying of a sacred thread traditional! In fact, even during India's freedom struggle many women tied the '*raksha sutra*' to protect the lives of the freedom fighters! It seems this tradition has been coming down since the *Vedic times*! On this day, there is a lot of excitement. Especially amongst girls who look forward to nice gifts from their brothers! Markets are full of dazzling *raakhis*. A variety of sweetmeats grace *mithai* shop counters.

GANESH CHATURTHI

Savita took a pinch of vermillion and touched her forehead, making a small dot. Then, she folded her hands in obeisance to the elephant deity at the altar of the temple she was visiting. The *pundit* (priest) rang a bell and chanted a prayer before giving her *prasaad*. Savita pulled her sari *pallu* tighter over her head and without turning her face away from the alter, she started moving backwards. She did not turn till she had reached the temple entrance. "I have to offer Ganpati milk and laddoos tomorrow," thought Savita to herself, "as it is Ganesh Chaturthi!" Savita mused as her foot trailed her *chappals* lying outside. Finally, she managed to get them on her feet. Muttering in her mother tongue, Marathi, "Ganapati Bappa Moriya, Pudhachya varshi lavkar ya" (meaning - Return early next year, O Victorious Lord Ganesh), Savita walked down the path towards her home.

Who is **Ganapati** and what is **Ganesh Chaturthi**?

Ganesh also known as Ganapati, is the **elephant- headed Hindu God**. He is the son of Shiv and Parvati.

Ganesh Chaturthi is the festival celebrated on the fourth day of the *Shukla Paksha* in the month of *Bhadrapad* (August-September).

It is said that on this day, Lord Ganesh was born and was declared first amongst the Gods.

For the Hindu, this day is of great importance! Hindus believe in praying to Ganesh who is considered the **remover of all obstacles** and the bestower of good fortune. In India, this festival is celebrated with great fervour in the state of Maharashtra, where it is also called **Vinayak Chaturthi.**

Savita entered her gate and made sure to distribute *prasaad* to the servant sweeping her courtyard. "I shall be sitting on the chair under the tree and reading," said Savita, "so get me a cup of tea, please." Picking up a book titled 'The Legends of Ganesh', Savita started to read.

'The Story of the birth of Ganesh', said the first chapter. Savita sighed and began to read, 'Legends say that Parvati created a beautiful boy from the dirt of her body, treated him as her son and gave him the responsibility of guarding her home.

Shiv, her husband did not know about this and when he came home he was confronted and challenged by the 'boy' created by his wife Parvati. The boy refused to let Shiv into his own home! Shiv became very angry and a clash ensued. The fall out was that Shiv chopped the boy's head off! When Parvati got to know of this, she was very angry with Shiv and later burst into tears. Seeing Parvati's condition, Shiv was filled with guilt and remorse at his wrong doing. He immediately sent his soldiers to the forest to bring the head of the first being they see sleeping facing north. The soldiers came across an elephant. Thus, an elephant head was brought and placed on the life less boy. With his new elephant head, the boy came alive and he became Ganesh! Ganesh is regarded by one and all, as the remover of obstacles, and he should be offered worship first, before any form of worship is offered to any other Gods.'

Savita turned to the second chapter. There was a nice story about Ganesh there. "Once on his birthday, Ganesh stuffed himself with lots of laddoos! Later with a bulging tummy he went for a ride on his vehicle, that is a mouse!

Yes, a mouse is considered to be his vehicle for transportation!

Why a mouse? Because a mouse can run very fast.

But then, a snake abruptly came in the way, startling the poor mouse. Ganesh toppled and his stomach burst open spilling all the laddoos out! Embarrassed, he quickly tied his stomach using the snake as a belt! Just then, Ganesh suddenly noticed the moon high up in the sky, laughing loudly. Ganesh became very angry and cursed the moon for laughing at his plight. He declared that on this day no one would look at him! So, as a rule, no one looks at the moon on Ganesh Chaturthi!"

Savita smiled reading on, 'Some say that Ganesh, in his anger, broke a bit of his tusk and hurled it at the moon. That is why in all idols of Ganesh, one of

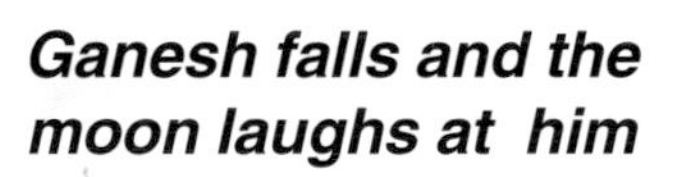
Ganesh falls and the moon laughs at him

his tusks is broken! Yet, others claim that he broke his tusk when he helped sage *Ved Vyasa* write the *Mahabharata*. Ganesh used a piece of his tusk to write the couplets!'

Savita closed the book and accepted the cup of tea the servant had brought. Reclining back on her chair under the tree, she sipped her tea and thought about the excitement and fervour that Ganesh Chaturthi would generate! The festivities include raising money and funds for charity, sculpting a variety of idols of Ganesh, music, dance and feasts. It would seem like the whole world had come alive! Huge, heavily decorated idols of Ganesh in clay, would

Celebration of Ganesh Chaturthi

be placed on high platforms. A brightly dressed priest would sing hymns and recite verses from the *Vedas*. Dancing and singing would take place. All sorts of games and gatherings would develop, adding to the air of festivity! Electric lights would string the idols blinking beautifully into the nights! Laddoos would make rounds! Laddoos would also be placed at all corners of the house and eaten before the meal! Sweet- meats are distributed too! Milk would be offered to idols! Visits to temples and family prayers were a must! These festivities would actually stretch over ten days!

On this day, students place books in front of the Ganesh idol and pray. They pray to the deity to sharpen their intelligence! That is why Ganesh is also known as '*one who grants intelligence*'.

Then, on the last day, a large procession (huge gathering of people) would carry the clay idols of Ganapati towards a river or sea and immerse it! The significance being that Ganesh was being given a farewell amidst much fanfare

as he made his way back to his abode in Kailash, taking away all the bad luck of man with him! In the procession, people would be chanting "Ganapati bappa moriya..!", also offering flowers, camphor and coconut!

Savita closed her eyes and let the feeling of contentment cover her. Yes she was looking forward to Ganesh Chaturthi and the thought that it was beginning tomorrow made her very happy indeed!

JANAMASHTAMI

"The eighth child of your sister Devaki and her husband Vasudeva shall be responsible for your death!" warned a voice from the skies. The ruler of Mathura, King Kansa, was enraged. "What? Her child will kill me? The invincible Kansa? Ha, not possible!" He stormed back to the palace.

Unknown to King Kansa, the Gods in heavens had earlier approached Lord Vishnu with their plea, "Dear Lord, do something. Put a stop to Kansa's cruelties! The wicked Kansa has snatched the kingdom from his father Ugrasena! His terrible atrocities on his subjects are horrifying! Mankind is suffering!" Lord Vishnu listened to their pleas. He decided to take his eighth incarnation and descend on earth.

He was to be born to Devaki and Vasudeva as their son. Unfortunately, Kansa was apprised of this by the voice in the sky!

That is why King Kansa was blazing with fury. Raising his sword, he attempted to behead his sister, "Aha, with you dead, how can your child be born!" he roared. Vasudeva stalled Kansa's attempt by imploring, "Please, do not kill her!"

King Kansa hears the oracle from the sky

Vasudeva carrying baby Krishna to the city of Gokul

"Why? How else can I save myself?" Kansa bellowed.

"Please spare her. I promise, whichever children are born to us, you may take them at birth!" Vasudeva beseeched. Kansa agreed and Devaki and her husband Vasudeva were locked up in a jail cell in a village near Mathura. One after the other, their six children succumbed to Kansa's wrath.

By divine intervention, Devaki's seventh child was transferred into the womb of Rohini, Vasudeva's first wife in Gokul, near Mathura. Kansa was told that Devaki had lost her seventh child. This child was born as *Balrama*, an incarnation of *Sheshnaga,* in Gokul. When the eighth child was born to Vasudeva and Devaki, the prison doors opened themselves and the guards fell into a deep sleep. The baby was born on a rainy and windy night at the stroke of twelve. Vasudeva and Devaki realised that this was no ordinary baby.

The baby wore silk robes and a radiant crown! The glow from the crown filled the cell! For some moments, Devaki and Vasudeva saw Lord Vishnu in his true form through the new-born baby. But not for long. That is because the vision quickly dispelled and the baby became a normal and ordinary one. But their surprises had not ended yet. Suddenly, a voice from the skies boomed "Vasudeva, carry this child across the river Yamuna to Gokul where Nanda lives. His wife Yashodha has given birth to a baby girl just now! Replace your son with the girl and come back here!" Vasudeva obeyed immediately. Placing the child in a wicker basket and carrying it on his head, Vasudeva walked his way through rain and wind. He stepped into the turbulent waters of Yamuna river. The blinding storm however was making it impossible for Vasudeva to proceed. Abruptly a cobra sprung up from the raging waters. This was *Ananta*, Lord Vishnu's serpent. The cobra spread its hood like an umbrella protecting Vasudeva and his baby from the torrential rains!

Krishna kills Kansa

After reaching Gokul, Vasudeva explained the entire story to Nanda and his wife Yashoda. After hearing him out, Nanda gladly gave up his baby girl and promised to keep the exchange a secret. Vasudeva returned with the baby girl. Suddenly, the rain and wind calmed down too! When the girl cried, the guards woke up and informed the king. Kansa hurriedly came to kill the baby girl. But the little baby girl slipped from his hand and was transformed into *Yogmaya*, the *shakti* or energy aspect of Lord Vishnu. Meanwhile, Devaki and Vasudeva's son grew up in Nanda and Yashoda's home. He was called Krishna. Krishna is the eighth of the ten incarnations of Lord Vishnu, the Preserver of the Universe. All through his child hood, Krishna performed amazing miracles! When Krishna grew up he killed Kansa, thus putting an end to his uncle's evil rule.

Devotees pulling strings to rock the baby Krishna in the cradle

Janamashtami is a festival celebrating the birth of Lord Krishna! Janam means 'birth' and 'ashtami' means eighth day. Since this day falls on the eighth day of a lunar fortnight, so his birthday is called *Janamashtami*! Janamashtami is celebrated on the eighth day of the *Krishna Paksha* in the month of *Bhadrapad* (August-September). It is celebrated with great fervour and gaiety in the states of Uttar Pradesh, Maharashtra and other northern states.

Krishna temples all over the world celebrate this day with vibrant enthusiasm! Devotees observe a fast on this day. Fasting and meditating on Janamastami is supposed to completely still all senses so that the divine Lord can show his presence. The temples are decorated on this occasion with tableau depicting scenes of Krishna's birth, his miraculous transfer to Gokul and his childhood pranks. An idol of Krishna in his *bal* or baby form is kept in a cradle and the devotees take turns pulling its string to rock the baby krishna.

At the stroke of twelve bells chime, conches blow and loud sounds of *"Hare Krishna"* fill the air. This is to announce the birth of the lord. Sweet-meats prepared from milk and curd are eaten. You know why? Well Krishna loved milk and curd! That is why earlier in the day a game called *'dahi handi'* is played! A large clay pot filled with curd, milk, honey, butter and fruits is hung at an inaccessible height. Then, young boys and men come forward for reaching the handi. They form a human pyramid by standing on each others' shoulders and don't stop till they have reached the pot! They break it and claim the contents! When the 'human pyramid' is being built, the others splash water and good-humouredly jeer, trying to make the task of the climbers as difficult as possible! This way, the victory of good over evil is celebrated exuberantly in this colourful and vibrant festival.

The game of 'dahi handi'

ONAM

The Gods come to lord Vishnu for help

Once upon a time, there lived a demon king called **Mahabali**. He ruled the kingdom of what is the state of modern day **Kerala** today. Mahabali was unlike all other demon kings! He was truthful and polite. His kingdom lived in peace with no fear or terror. Only unity and happiness! Alas! This made the Gods or the *devas* unhappy.

"We have no domination on the earth, sky and space!" they complained amongst themselves. "King Bali, through intense prayer and penance has gained total control of the three worlds and we have nothing left!"

The Gods decided to do something about it. They approached Lord Vishnu with their protest.

Lord Vishnu listened to their problem and realized that something had to be done. He knew that King Bali was a wonderful king and his people adored him; however, the Gods needed their areas of domination too, *so as to create a balance*! Lord Vishnu decided to come to Earth himself to solve the problem.

He took birth in the home of sage Kashyapa and Aditi. That is how Lord Vishnu took his fourth incarnation in the form of a dwarf! He called himself **Vamana**! When he grew up, he visited the court of the demon King Bali. There was a sacrifice being performed there. Mahabali identifying Vamana as a visiting Brahmin, asked him what he desired! Vamana got his chance! Vamana asked "O great king, can I please have three feet of land to live in!"

Highly amused, the demon king agreed saying, "Yes, you may have three feet of land anywhere in my kingdom!"

Suddenly, Vamana expanded to a very large size! Taking one step, he covered the entire earth. With the next step he covered the sky. By now, Bali realized that the dwarf was not an ordinary being! So, just as Vamana was putting his third foot down, Bali put his head under it to get salvation. His head was pushed to the nether worlds! There, he asked the dwarf to reveal his true identity. Poof!! The dwarf disappeared and instead stood Lord Vishnu! Overjoyed to see Lord Vishnu, the demon king bowed in obeisance! Lord Vishnu said, "You have been a good and virtuous king Mahabali so you may ask me for a boon!"

Mahabali told the lord that he loved his people very much so he wanted permission to visit Kerala once in a year. Lord Vishnu immediately granted his wish! So, once a year on this day, King Bali visits Kerala. His homecoming is celebrated as **Onam**. This festival is celebrated on the twelfth day of the waning moon in the month of *Bhadrapad* (August-September).

King Bali gets salvation from Vishnu disguised as Vamana

To welcome their king, Kerala comes alive during Onam! Homes are decorated with fresh flowers. King Mahabali is welcomed with a 'pookalam' or flower mat! This is a must for every home!

Everybody in the family buys new clothes. Scrumptious sweetmeats and great vegetarian dishes are served on banana leaves. One such delicious sweet dish is *payasam*.

Traditional rituals are performed too. During this festival, Kerala sees a colourful parade of elephants and fireworks. For entertainment, the popular Indian dance, **'Kathakali'** is also staged. **'Vallamkali'** or the boat race is a famous

Vallamkali or boat race

attraction during Onam. The most famous is the *snake boat* race! Here, the boats are shaped like snakes and has over a hundred oarsmen!

They all row together and sing the song of the boatman in a chorus! This is considered the largest team sport in the world! Various types of other boats also take part in this popular event. Teams are formed and crowds throng the waterside to cheer their favourite teams!

Women also take part in independent events too! The race begins with a colourful pageant of decorated floats resounding with dances and songs!

Onam is also a harvest festival! Kerala, after three months of heavy rains, welcomes the sun and the good weather! Kerala also rejoices for it is the time to reap a healthy harvest after months of toil and labour.

NAVRATRI & DURGA PUJA

'Navratri' are nine auspicious days which are celebrated as the days of Goddess Durga. This festival occurs twice a year , at the change from winter to summer in the Spring, and again at the change from summer to winter in the Autumn. The Autumn festival is celebrated from the first day to the ninth day of the bright half of *Ashwin* (September-October), while the Spring festval is celebrated in *Chaitra* (April-May). The two Navaratri celebrations are known as *Ram-Navaratri* in *Chaitra* and *Durga Navaratri* in *Ashwin*. This is the time to worship Goddess Durga. She is seen in nine different forms. Amongst her many forms, one sees her as **Goddess Lakshmi** for peace and prosperity and another as **Goddess Saraswati**, the Goddess of knowledge. Why do we celebrate Navratri and worship Goddess Durga? Well, it is believed that on this day, Goddess Durga killed the demon **Mahishasura** and rid the world of his evils. Actually, it all began when Mahishasura prayed very, very hard to become invincible! Alas, this power made him arrogant. "I am unbeatable!" he roared to the *Devas* or Gods.

The *Devas* were unable to match his invincibility and Mahishasura managed to seize *Devaloka*, the heavenly abode of the Gods! So, the *Devas* came together and created **Durga** from their combined energies. They wanted Durga to take on the challenge of vanquishing Mahishasura!

"Oh, great divine mother, Ma Durga," said the *Devas*. "You are *Shakti*, the result of all our strengths! Destroy this indestructible enemy!"

Goddess Durga looked awesome. She was astride a lion in shimmering red apparel, with significant weapons in her four hands. "I shall put an end to the terror spread by Mahishasura!" Durga promised the Gods. The battle between Mahishasura and Durga went on for nine days! Finally, Durga or 'Ma Shakti' trampled Mahishasura to death!

Goddess Durga killing Mahishasura

In northern India, a dry coconut is covered with a red cloth and placed on a small pot in the *puja ghar*, symbolising the Goddess. Then, a few jowar seeds are planted in a pot and kept near it. Generally, the ladies of the house fast for nine days and consume only special **Navratra food**. On the eighth or the ninth day, i.e. on *Ashtami* or *Navami,* they make *suji halwa*, *puris* and *chanas* for *prasad*. They feed seven or nine young girls as the Goddess is worshipped in the form of a *kanya* or girl.

Woman praying to Goddess Durga

In Bengal, it is called 'Durga Puja'. Day and night celebrations take place. This is a time for complete festivity for them. During Durga Puja, beautiful idols of the Mother Goddess are worshipped on grand stages or *pandals* for those nine days. Goddess Durga's images here depicts a valiant ten-handed Goddess siting on a lion, holding a trident and killing the demon Mahishasura lying at her feet.

Dandiya

On the ninth day, the idols are transported out in a procession to be immersed in a river or pond! The making of the idols also has some rules! The rules being that whatever goes into the making of these idols should have come out of the river *Ganga* (Ganges)! So, the idols are shaped with the fine clay from the bed of the Ganges. This river is revered and considered to be the giver of life especially in West Bengal! That is why after nine days these idols are immersed into a nearby river or ocean, signifying the coming of a full cycle!

Navratri is also celebrated as a festival of nine auspicious nights in Gujarat. The most important feature of the Gujarat Navaratri's are the dances! The Dandiya and the Garba dance shapes the most important activity during this festival. It is performed with great gusto by both men and women! Sticks click in musical synchronization to swift circular movements! These movements have both auspicious and magical connotations! The festival is thus celebrated in different parts of India under different names but the underlying thought is the same, i.e. worship of Goddess Durga.

DUSSEHRA

Ram kills Ravan

Dussehra falls on the tenth day of the waxing moon in the month of *Ashwin* (September-October). This festival celebrates the victory of Lord Ram, the prince of Ayodhya, over the mighty ruler of Lanka, the ten-headed demon king Ravan.

Why did Lord Ram kill Ravan? Well, the story goes like this: Lord Ram was in exile in the forest with his wife Sita and brother Lakshman. There Ravan's sister Surupnakha saw them and approached Ram to marry her. When Ram refused, Surupnakha attacked Sita to kill her. To stop her from harming Sita, Lakshman chopped off her nose. To avenge his sister's insult, Ravan in the guise of a *rishi* or a sage kidnapped Sita.

Lord Ram with his brother Laxman gathered an army from the forest itself and waged a victorious ten-day war in order to get Sita back! Dussehra marks the culmination of this war and the destruction of Ravan. That is why Dussehra is also called as **Vijayadashmi** as it celebrates the victory of good over evil. Dussehra or *Dasha-hara* means 'victory over the ten-faced one!'

Ravan is depicted as the evil king of *Rakshasas* or demons. But was he such an evil being? In truth, it is speculated that King Ravan was not all bad. He was a great scholar! It also must be remembered that Ravan was a dedicated devotee of Lord Shiv. He was given special powers too! But Ravan misused the powers given to him which led to his destruction and he came to be called evil!

Effigies of Ravan, Kumbhkarna and Meghnath are burnt

The festival of Dussehra has a message for all to expel the wrong habits and actions and follow the path of truth and righteousness.

In northern India, the nine days preceding Dussehra are known as Navratri and the episodes from Lord Ram's life are staged in the form of *Ram Leela*. What happens on Dussehra day? On Dussehra day, huge effigies or dummies personifying **Ravan**, his brother **Kumbhkarna** and son **Meghnath** are created. They are positioned in vast open grounds! The rerun of the drama by actors shows a grand finale of Ram, accompanied by his consort Sita and his brother Lakshman arriving at the battle-ground! Ram and Lakshman shoot fire arrows at the dummies. The effigies are stuffed with firecrackers! When the crackers catch fire, there is a deafening boom and the effigies blow up signifying successfully the victory of good over evil!"

Dussehra is also celebrated with much aplomb in the city of Mysore. Here a grand procession is taken out on magnificent bedecked elephants.

Dussehra also marks the end of the Navratri period, leading to the immersion of images of Goddess Durga in the waters of the nearest river or ocean.

KARVA CHAUTH

Married woman praying to Shiv and Parvati

Nine days before Diwali, the festival of **Karva Chauth** is celebrated! This festival is celebrated in Punjab, Rajasthan, Uttar Pradesh and Gujarat. Women keep a fast on this day and only break it on sighting the moon! They pray to the Moon God asking for the well-being and long life of their husbands.

On the eve of this festival, women wear *mehendi* or henna on their palms, hands and feet! Bangles, anklets, toe rings, bindis, vermilion and what ever signifies the status of a married woman, shapes the fashion of the day too! Markets are full as women buy stuff for this festival. They buy new *karvas* or clay pots too. Mother-in-laws buy '*sargi*' for their daughter-in-laws. All things in the *sargi* are meant to bring good fortune for the receiver.

On Karva Chauth, the day starts early for women. Before sunrise, women bathe and pray to Shiv and Parvati, hoping that their own married lives will be as successful as that of the divine couple. A hearty meal is partaken before sunrise too! After that, the fasting women eat nothing and do not even drink a drop of water till they see the moon in the evening. Early evening, a small ceremonious ritual takes place. The women offer prayers to Goddess Parvati asking for long, healthy lives for their husbands. Then they pass around individual *thalis* (plates) in which *baya* is kept. *Baya* is a traditional offering of almonds, *mathris* (short crust pastry) and small gifts. Every one carries a small *karva* of water too. This is placed in the center of the *thali*. *Diyas* made of clay or *atta* are lit and placed on the *thali* too. After the *puja*, this thali minus the karvas and diyas, is given to the eldest member of the family. During the passing of the *thalis*, the story of Karva Chauth is narrated:

Veeravati with Shiv and Parvati

Once upon a time, there lived a beautiful princess by the name of Veeravati. She had seven brothers who loved her dearly. Soon, Veerawati married a king. On Karva Chauth, Veeravati went to her brothers' place. She was fasting. By the evening, she was almost faint with hunger. But the moon was taking its time in coming out. Her brothers persuaded her to eat something. "Please brothers," said Veerawati, "I will only eat after I see the moon."

"Oh dear, we cannot see our sister suffer like this!" the brothers fretted in anxiety. "I have an idea," whispered one brother excitedly. 'Let us create a moon!"

And that's what they did! Unknown to Veeravati, they cleverly created a false moon by burning a fire far away. Believing them, Veerawati broke her fast. As soon as she had eaten, she received the terrible news that her husband was dead! A devastated Veerawati rushed to the palace. On her way, she met Lord Shiv and his consort, Goddess Parvati.

Veeravati begged them to grant her husband his life back!

"You have come too late Veeravati!" said the Goddess. "You saw a false moon and insulted the reasons for keeping the fast!"

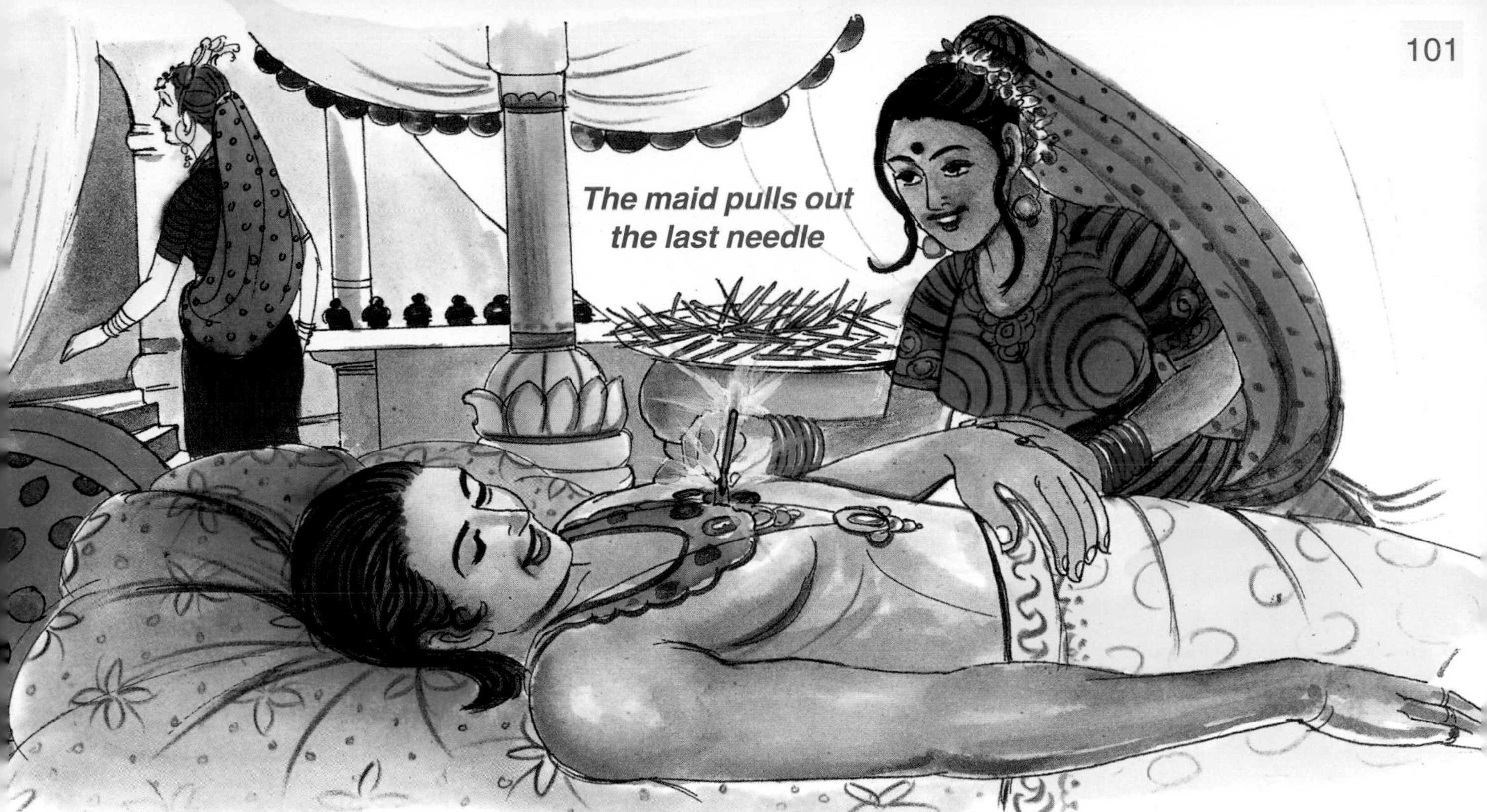

"Oh, divine mother! Pardon me this sin. Please tell me what I can do to bring back my husband?" sobbed Veeravati.

Taking pity on her, the Goddess said, "Go home! You will find your husband alive!" Veeravati bowed gratefully and hurriedly got up to leave.

"Wait!" said Goddess Parvati. "He shall be alive, but covered with thousands of needles. Pluck the needles carefully, till there are no needles left and he will be fine. That is your punishment!" said the Goddess.

True enough, on reaching the palace, Veeravati found the king alive but unconscious. His body had thousands of needles piercing it.

Veerawati painstakingly cared for her husband. Daily, she picked out hundreds of needles from his unconscious body. The year passed and it was Karva Chauth again. With utmost caution and devotion, Veeravati kept the fast. Now, there was only one needle left in her husband's body. Stepping out for a few minutes, Veeravati planned to come back and take out the final needle. However, before she could come back, her maid chancing upon the king, plucked out the last needle!

On regaining consciousness, the king mistook the maid to be his queen!

Poor Veeravati found herself restricted to the servant quarters. Sad and woeful, she watched as her maid enjoyed royal status, which was rightfully hers. Then, one day while passing, the king stopped by Veeravati. As a king inquires of his subjects, he asked her if she needed anything.

"Sire, please give me two identical dolls." said Veerawati

On receiving the dolls, Veeravati begin to sing, "*Rani thi Jo Goli ho gayi, Goli thi Jo Rani ho gayi!*" (the maid is the queen and the queen is the maid). The king became curious on hearing this. He asked her what she meant. Veeravati told him the entire story. On hearing her story, the king instantly remembered her and Veeravati was immediately restored to her correct place.

So, this story reminds us to respect the bonds of matrimony and the bonds of commitments! It is told and retold on every Karva Chauth.

What happens when the moon is sighted? The sighting of the moon is another exciting event. Everyone eagerly awaits for it to rise. When the moon comes out, the women offer it water from the *karva* and sweetmeats seven times, praying alongside. They place the lit diya on a sieve *(chhanni)* and see the moon. Then immediately, they also see their husband's face through the lit sieve. After this, they take their first sip of water from the *karvas*, to break their fast. Many a times, husbands present their wives with a piece of jewelry or a gift after sighting of the moon! Karva Chauth is celebrated with the same fervour wherever it is observed. Though with a little difference in tradition of course! However, the underlying meaning of this festival remains the same. That is, a prayer from married women for a healthy and prosperous long life for their husbands.

Woman looking at husband's face through the sieve

In Hindi, Deepavali literally means a 'row of lamps' and Diwali as it is popularly known, means the 'festival of light'! We celebrate Diwali in the month of *Kartik* (October-November) on the darkest moonless night or *Amavasya*! It is the main festival of many Hindus and celebrated with lights, crackers, sweets and feasts throughout India. Prayers are offered to invoke the blessings of **Goddess Lakshmi**, the Hindu *Goddess of Wealth*. It marks the coming of winters and the beginning of a new year for the people of Gujarat, the *Marwaris* and businessmen.

Worship of Goddess Lakshmi

This festival actually starts from the thirteenth day of the waning moon in *Kartik* and goes on till the *dooj* or the second day of the waxing moon. There are five days of Diwali. Each day has a special significance.

The **first day** is called **Dhanteras**. This day is very important for the business community of India. '*Dhan*' means wealth and '*teras*', the thirteenth day of the Hindu month. According to ancient Indian medicine science, or *Ayurveda*, it is the birthday of the **Lord Dhanwantari**! He is the God who grants immortality. On this day, people pray for lots of money and success in the year. Lord Dhanwantari was the divine physician, so people worship him as a symbol of good health on this day! People generally buy new utensils or metal objects as auspicious items, which they believe will ward off evil and ill health for the rest of the year and bring peace and prosperity.

However, there is another noteworthy reason for this day! **God Yam**, the *God of Death*, is worshipped on this day to provide prosperity and well being to people. There is a story behind this.

Years ago, King Hima was a worried man. As per horoscope predictions, his 16 years old son was doomed to die on the fourth day of his marriage by snakebite!

"The poor prince," cried everyone, "he is fated to die!"

But the prince's wife would have none of that! On the fourth day of their marriage, she lit countless oil *diyas* all over the place. She also heaped ornaments and gold and silver coins at the entrance of the prince's chambers! Then, in a lovely lilting sing song way, the princess went on telling stories to her prince. Meanwhile, *Yam*, the God of death, disguised himself as a snake and slithered to the prince's room! But he could not enter the prince's room! Why? The snake was blinded by the bright lights of the *diyas* and the ornaments! The snake halted in his tracks. Faintly melodious songs floated to him.

"What are those sounds coming from inside the chambers?" thought the snake. That was actually the princess singing to her prince. *Yam* was curious. He went closer. Drawn to the wonderful musical notes, he slithered atop the stack of ornaments. Soon, Yam was lost to the mesmerizing tunes! He sat there through out the night and quietly left in the morning; without harming the prince! Since then, *Dhan-Teras* came to be known as the day of 'Yamadeepaan'! Lamps are kept lit throughout the night in respect to *Yam*, the God of Death, to prevent untimely deaths!

Yam disguised as a snake listening to the songs sung by the princess

Satyabhama killing Narakasura

The **second day** of Diwali is called **Naraka Chaturdashi** or *chhoti Diwali*! The legend goes that on this day Lord Krishna destroyed the demon Narakasur and made the world free from his terror! **Narakasura** was the son of Goddess Earth and had a demonic bent of mind.

He liked to live in filth and was destructive by nature. He harassed the Gods living in the heaven as well as the saints praying on earth! One day, he overthrew the king of Suraloka called Aditi. More over, he carried away 16,000 women and imprisoned them in his palace! Aditi was the relative of Satyabhama, Lord Krishna's wife!

"This is outrageous!" cried the Gods! "Shame on Narakasura!"

"Yes sire, this is terrible indeed!" agreed Lord Krishna's wife Satyabhama.

Satyabhama pleaded to her husband Krishna, "Please, dear husband, give me a chance to vanquish this evil demon!" Krishna thought deeply and then replied, "All right, dear wife. You may vanquish Narakasura. But, on the battle ground, I shall be your charioteer!"

With Krishna as the charioteer, Satyabhama entered the battle-field. During the war, Krishna pretended to faint thus giving his wife a chance to behead the monster! Narakasura was killed and once again, good prevailed over evil. This event is celebrated with much rejoicing, especially in southern India and Assam. Lamps are lit as a mark of celebration. On this day, houses are washed, painted and decorated; all filth is discarded. Children light crackers, eat sweets and generally have fun on this day.

The **third day** is considered **actual Diwali**! It is on this day that Lord Ram, Lord Vishnu's seventh incarnation, returned to his city Ayodhya with his wife Sita, after killing the Lankan ruler Ravan. Lord Ram had been exiled for fourteen years and the people of Ayodhya welcomed him with lights and flowers. It is also an important day because this is the only day of the year, when **Goddess Lakshmi** comes down to earth. People perform **Lakshmi Puja** (worship of Goddess Lakshmi) on Diwali, seeking wealth and prosperity for the whole year. People are even expected to take a traditional oil bath and be very, very clean!

Prior to Diwali, homes are painted, white washed, spring cleaned and made sparkling clean. For Deepavali day, new clothes and gifts are purchased for near and dear ones! Markets are well lit and are full of festivities! People visit each other and give gifts. Diwali is bonanza time for business people, because it is the maximum time for giving gifts and making maximum purchases. New account books or *bahis* are also inaugurated on this day. In Bengal, Diwali is celebrated as the day for *Kali Puja*.

After sunset, people perform the *Lakshmi Puja* seeking wealth and prosperity for the whole year. People firmly believe that the Goddess Lakshmi would visit their homes and bestow prosperity and good fortune on them on Diwali days! Also, since Diwali falls during a dark period of the year, it is advised that the best way to drive out damaging influences of darkness is to light candles, *diyas* etc! So on all the five days of Diwali, homes glitter with electric light bulbs and even oil lamps sometimes!

'Patakas' or fire works are an integral part of Deepavali. Children especially, burst crackers celebrating the victory of good over evil! It is also said that crackers represent the fiery weapons used by Lord Krishna to defeat Narakasura! Diwali dispels the darkness of evil with the brightness of lights!

In our present age, there is a monitored control on fire-crackers though. Do you know why? Because what started off as tame fun, has turned into

Lord Ram returns to Ayodhya

dangerous foolhardiness. Nowadays, the crackers are quite badly made. There are many 'burn' accidents taking place. No one takes precautions handling crackers and silly mistakes prove fatal. The worst thing is that children are used in the factories to make crackers. Most factories are breaking fire safety laws and polluting our environment badly. People are actually getting sick with the haze and pollution that crackers create! That is why the campaign against crackers is speeding up and currently most children say, 'No to firecrackers!'

The day after Diwali is known as **Annakoot**. On this day, *Govardhan* mountain or the mountain of food is worshipped. According to a legend, when Lord krishna was a young boy, he asked the people of Gokul to worship Govardhan mountain instead of Lord Indra, who is the giver of rain. When the people shifted their focus of prayers from Lord Indra to Govardhan, Indra flew into a rage.

"How dare they do this!" thundered Indra. With one mighty spell, he sent a deluge of rain and storm for seven days to drown Gokul. Krishna saved Gokul by lifting and holding the Govardhan mountain over the people like an umbrella! He lifted the mountain on his little finger so that the people and cattle could come beneath it to seek refuge from the rains. Govardhan provided them with food and water for these seven days. Thus, the day after Diwali is celebrated as **Govardhan Puja**.

Workers celebrate this day as **Vishwakarma Puja** also and worship their tools and machinery.

The **fifth and final day** of Diwali Festival is known by the name of **Bhai Dooj.** This day is observed as a symbol of love between sisters and brothers. It is believed that on this day, *Yamraj*, the God of death, visited his sister *river Yamuna* and she put 'tilak' on his forehead! Tilak is a holy dot put on the forehead with flower petals, milk, saffron, turmeric and vermilion! On this day, sister apply *tika* on their brother's forehead and get gifts and blessings in return.

Diwali thus assumes immense importance for the people of India. It is eagerly awaited by both young and old as it is the time for family celebrations, feasting and exchange of gifts.

Krishna lifts the Govardhan mountain

CHHAT PUJA

Chhat Puja is an important festival in eastern India, especially in the state of Bihar. It comes six days after Deepavali. This festival is basically a thanks giving to the Sun God, *Surya*! The duration of this festival is two days and is usually celebrated in the month of *Kartik* (October-November).

On the first day, a fast is kept. Before the fast, devotees have a bath or holy cleansing. The fast is broken in the evening after a family prayer session in front of the temple at home. Seasonal fruits and special delicacies are offered as 'prasaad'. These are shared amongst all family members.

On the second day, devotees actually camp on the banks of the river. The day starts with a twenty-four hour fast. The women of the house spruce up their kitchens squeaky clean and make a 'prasad' to offer the divine Sun God. The freshly harvested crop of wheat and rice becomes the main ingredients in the *prasaad*. The sweet meats prepared as offerings are supposed to be the favourites of Lord Surya so the cooking is done with strict supervision. The lady in charge, abstains from wearing clothes that are stitched and refuses to eat cooked meals. No one can enter this kitchen without a bath.

Woman praying to Sun God

Men folk sit outside the house on guard. Later, they guard the baskets of *prasaad* at the riverside.

The women folk carry six baskets containing food, flowers and clay elephants as an offering to the Sun God, to the nearest river or lake. Hands holding the basket are held up so as to not contaminate the offering by touch. Then, they stand in the water for many hours chanting *mantras* and paying obeisance to lord Surya. They keep on standing in water, be it a cold day or hot and the offerings remain immersed in water. Some women undertake even harder vows if their wishes are fulfilled. There is no priest to conduct the ceremony. After immersion, the food is considered blessed and then the women who had been starving, consume it first as the *prasaad* of lord Surya. Later it is distributed to everyone. Large fairs are also organised along the river front, with different stalls of food and entertainment. This festival fosters the spirit of community worship, sharing and perseverance.

GURPURAB

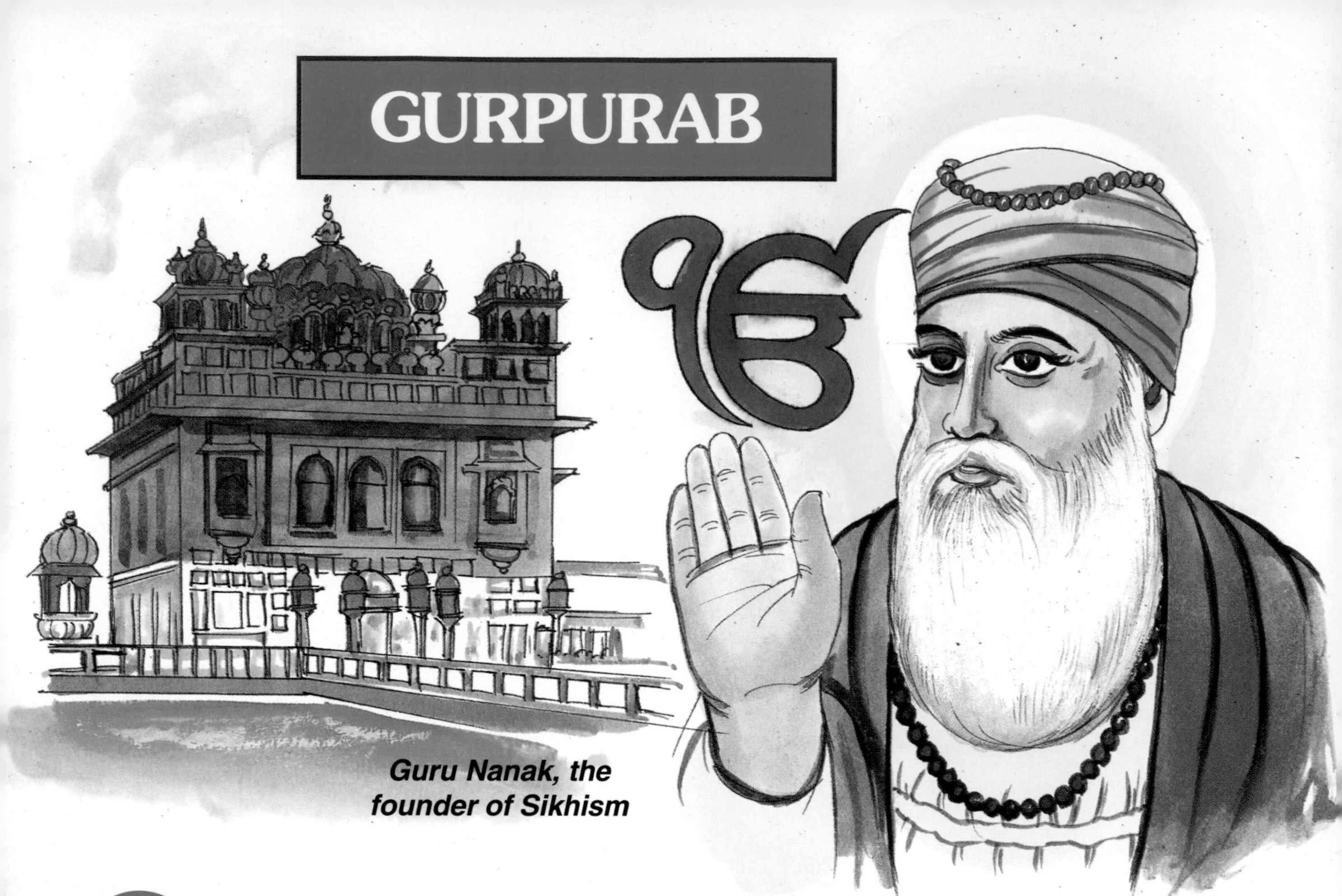

Guru Nanak, the founder of Sikhism

Gurpurab is one of the important Sikh festivals. The Sikhs celebrate ten Gurpurabs in a year. Each Gurpurab marks either the birth, death or martyrdom days of the Sikh Gurus. The most significant Gurpurab is that of the birth anniversary of the first Sikh Guru, Guru Nanak. It is also called as **Guru Nanak Jayanti** and is celebrated in the month of *Kartik* (November).

Guru Nanak was the founder of Sikhism. He was born to Mehta Kalu and Mata Tripata in the village of Talwandi, in Lahore in Pakistan. Even as a child, Guru Nanak was different from other children. He carried around him a divine aura. When he grew up, he devoted his life to the welfare of people. He spread a message of love and tolerance. His message knew no boundaries of sect, caste or religion. Guru Nanak said that a man of religion should do three things. **Firstly**, he should earn his living with honest labour and should not lead an idle life. **Secondly**, he should share his earnings with others and help the weak. **Thirdly**, he should always remember God and should ask others to do likewise.

Fifteen days before Gurunanak Jayanti, the uninterrupted reading of the holy book of the Sikhs, the 'Guru Granth Sahib' also begins. This is called *Akand Path*. It concludes on the day of Guru Nanak Jayanti. The Granth Sahib is then taken out in a procession. The holy book is beautifully decorated. Children along with adults, follow the procession singing hymns. Five guards who are called *'panj pyare'* walk along too. The Sikh flag flies at the head of the procession. Later in the day, people flock to the *Gurudwaras*. Special sessions of hymns and discourses are arranged there. After offering prayers, there is a community lunch. This is a free lunch and is called **langar**. Everyone takes turns in helping in anyway for a langar. Sikhs also distribute the traditional *'Karah Prasaad'* or *halwa* to everyone on this day. Homes and Gurudwaras are brightly lit up in the evening on this day. The main places of worship are the **Guru Nanaka Sahib** in Pakistan and the **Golden Temple** at Amritsar.

Sighting of the new moon

Id-ul-Fitr is the most auspicious festival for Muslims all over the world. The Muslim faith is called Islam. As the Hijri or Islamic calendar is based on the movements of the moon, the timings of this festival differ from year to year. The festival of Id-ul-Fitr marks the culmination of the holy month of *Ramzan*. It is celebrated on the first day of the next month, namely *Shawwal*, which starts when three people sight the new moon. Id-ul-Fitr marks the end of the month of fasting or *Roza*.

Muslims offering Namaz

It is believed that in the month of *Ramzan,* **Prophet Muhammad** (messenger of *Allah*) offered prayers to *Allah* or God in a secluded place, a cavern. He observed a fast or *roza* for this whole month, as a penance seeking forgiveness for the sins of mankind. He went on praying and meditating. During this period, the holy *Quran*, the Islamic religious book, was revealed to him by *Allah* and the prophet was asked to spread his message amongst people.

Every year, during the month of *Ramzan,* from sunrise to sunset, Muslims abstain from food and drink in a form of self-purification. They do not even drink water during the daytime. Praying, offering *namaz* and reading the *Quran* are the traditional rituals during *roza.* After the sunset, the fast or *roza* is broken with fruits and food. Pious Muslims believe that during *Ramzan,* the doors to paradise or *Jannat* are open and those of hell are closed. Those who fast believe that they will be forgiven for their sins and will be permitted to go to *Jannat.* However, old and sick people and pregnant women are exempted from doing *rozas*.

Children getting idi

Children eating sewaiyan

On Id-ul-Fitr, greetings of "Id-Mubarak" or "a blessed Eid" ring all around intermingled with the din created by happy laughter on this day. Id-ul-Fitr literally means breaking of fast. It is the third 'pillar' or religious obligation of Islam and also a way of coming closer to *Allah*. On this festive day, Muslims put on their best clothes and go to the mosque to pray. The Muslim form of prayer is called *'Namaz'*.

People also give alms or *zakaat* to the poor. After the rituals, the feasts and fairs start. *Sewaiyan*, a kind of sweet dish, is an important part of the feast. Gifts are also exchanged and elders give money, called *idi*, to children. It is a festival that brings gifts, feasts and joy. It combines the rituals and traditions of the religion with the fun and frolic of everyday life.

CHRISTMAS

Around December, "Merry Christmas" becomes a common greeting! Christmas is an important festival of the followers of the world's largest religion, **Christianity**. It is celebrated on the **twenty fifth of December** as the birthday of **Lord Jesus Christ**. Special prayers or a mass is held in the church for Christ, thus the name Christmas.

Jesus was born to Mary and Joseph. This was no ordinary birth! An angel had told Mary that she would have an extraordinary baby. Joseph did not believe her at first. Then, an angel told him in a dream that it was true! They had to travel from their home in Nazareth to Bethlehem (near Jerusalem), to index their names with the ruling Roman government.

Birth of Jesus Christ

Alas, at Bethlehem, there was no room for them to stay at any inn. The only place offered was the stable! You know the place were animals are kept! That is where Lord Jesus was born! When Jesus was born, there was no bed for him. So, they put him into an animal feed trough; laying dry hay for comfort! The birth of Jesus was announced to the shephard boys nearby by a bright light and a descending angel! When they were frightened, the angel assured them that a king was going to be born and this king would perform miracles and save them from evil! Also, three wise men followed a star shining in the sky carrying gifts of gold, frankincense and myrrh for the special birth, which was going to take place! They reached the place where Jesus was born following the star!

Since 400 AD, Christians have celebrated the birth of Jesus. 'Christ' means 'Messiah' or 'Anointed One'! Christians believe that Jesus was appointed by God to save the world from evil.

The celebrations for Christmas start from **Christmas Eve,** i.e., the twenty fourth of December. People go for Midnight Mass, sing hymns and carols in church. Churches are decorated with poinsettias (red star shaped flowers) and lit with candles for the Christmas Evening. The priest gives a sermon. The message in the sermons would be of love and salvation. People gather in good numbers to pray and thank god for his sacrifices that are believed to have saved mankind. Homes and *bazaars* are decorated, the main colours being red, green and white. Holly is placed at the entrance doors of homes.

Santa Clause

What is holly? It is a ring of green, intervened with tiny bells and artificial berries hanging at the door. Holly is associated as a symbol of good luck.

Holly

Some men dress up as Santa Claus or Father Christmas and distribute sweets or small gifts at markets. Who is Santa Claus?

St. Nicholas, the jolly plump man with a big sack and beard, dressed in red is called Father Christmas! He is supposed to be living in the North Pole! Father Christmas is based on a real person, St. Nicholas, which explains his other name 'Santa Claus' which comes from the Dutch word 'Sinterklaas'. Nicholas was supposed to be a Christian leader in the 4th century AD. He never wanted poor people to know he was helping them! So it seems one day, he climbed the roof of a house and dropped the purse of money down a chimney. Now a girl was drying her stocking by the fireplace and the money purse slipped right into her stocking!

That is why, it is believed that Father Christmas comes down the chimney and places gifts in children's stockings. He rumbles into houses with his bell jingling down the chimney at midnight! It is said that Santa Claus has a gift for every child all over the world! He works in his home in the North Pole and makes gifts with the help of elves! Santa Claus flies from the North Pole in a sledge drawn by reindeers! The sky is filled with his merry call which goes... “HO HO HO HO HO HO !”

Elves making gifts

Baby Jesus with the Fir tree

No Christmas celebration is complete without the Christmas tree! It is a day for family get-togethers and feasts are spread out under a bedecked and illuminated tree. The Christmas tree is associated with the birth of Jesus Christ. It is believed that on the night of the birth of Christ, all kinds of living creatures came to Bethlehem with gifts. The olive tree came along with its fruit and the palm with its date but the fir tree had nothing to gift baby Jesus. But an angel took pity on the fir tree and zapped a cluster of stars to shine on its beautiful boughs. Baby Jesus gurgled and smiled seeing the lighted tree and blessed it. So that is why, the fir tree is always lighted with many decorations on it, to please little children during Christmas. The tree has a silver star on its tip always. Bells and golden balls hung on its boughs. Electric lights strung in rows too.

Though the tree is supposed to be of fir, nowadays artificial ones are available too! It is also said that tree is evergreen and symbolizes health and prosperity!

The festival of Christmas is celebrated by children all over the world. Christmas parties are organized in classes and schools. Children hang up their stockings at night on Christmas eve in anticipation of gifts from Santa Claus. Christmas cards are also exchanged. Since there are only six more days left for the New Year, people wish each other "Merry Christmas and a Happy New Year." Fun, frolic and laughter mark this year-end festival.

Children enjoying a Christmas party